Edited by Gary Gillette

Kingston, New York

Produced in partnership with and licensed by
Major League Baseball Properties, Inc.
The Major League Baseball club insignias depicted in this product
are the exclusive property of the respective Major League Baseball clubs
and may not be reproduced without their written permission.

Minor League organization reports provided by Howe Sportsdata,
a service of SportsTicker/ESPN.

Photo credits:
Major League Baseball: 52 (bottom), 54
National Baseball Library: 59 (bottom), 69
Photo File: 52 (top), 56 (top), 59 (top), 79, 82 (bottom)
Transcendental Graphics: 43, 44, 45, 46, 47, 48, 49, 50, 51, 53, 55, 56 (bottom), 58, 60, 62, 65, 66, 67, 68, 70,
71, 72, 73, 75, 76, 77, 78, 80, 81, 82 (top), 84

Total Sports Publishing, Inc. books may be purchased for educational,
business or sales promotional use. For information please write to:
Total Sports Publishing, Inc.
100 Enterprise Drive
Kingston, NY 12401

Total Sports Publishing is a trademark of Total Sports, Inc. used under license.
Library of Congress Catalog Number: 00-100542
ISBN:1-892129-58-2
Printed in the United States of America
10 9 8 7 6 5 4 3 2 1
Cover design by Donna Harris
Book design by Sandy Coe

Tigers Team History

One of the more successful clubs in the American League, the Tigers have enjoyed winning seasons nearly 70 percent of the time. In 18 of their 61 winning seasons, they have remained in contention into the final days, 11 times emerging triumphant as league or division champions.

Detroit was one of the clubs from Ban Johnson's Western League that (renamed the American League) raised itself to major league status in 1901 with a talent raid on the long-established National League. In their first six big league seasons, the Tigers displayed little bite, finishing four times in the second division and never threatening for the league lead.

In 1907 all that changed. Sparked by a young right fielder, Ty Cobb (who in his first full big league season led the league in batting, slugging, hits, RBIs, and stolen bases) and led by a dynamic new manager, Hugh "Eeyah" Jennings (who knew enough not to try to tell Cobb how to play the game), the Tigers clawed their way to the pennant in a four-way race. The outcome might have been different if two late-season games with second-place Philadelphia had not been rained out. Today's rules would require that the games be made up.

The 1908 race was even closer, with four teams contending into late September. The race wasn't settled until the final day, when Detroit beat Chicago to edge Cleveland by half a game. Once again the pennant hinged on a rainout that had not been made up. And once again Cobb dominated the league's hitters (though he slipped to fourth in stolen bases).

The Tigers had a slightly easier time of it the next year. It was a three-way race into September, but Detroit then pulled away to finish 3 ½ games ahead of Philadelphia. Cobb, in his best season yet, took the Triple Crown and returned to the top in stolen bases. But the Tigers were again unable to win a World Series. In 1907, after an opening-game tie, the Chicago Cubs swept the next four. The Cubs lost Game 3 the next year, but won the other four. And in 1909 Pittsburgh and Detroit alternated victories, with the Pirates emerging world champions in seven games.

Jennings managed Detroit for 11 more seasons; then Cobb took the reins for six years before leaving for Philadelphia. But the Tigers won no more pennants in the Cobb era. Cobb himself continued to dominate the league offensively through 1919. In 1911 he achieved career highs in most offensive categories, including a batting average of .420, but the Tigers managed no better than a distant second to the Athletics. In 1915 they started strong and remained in the race throughout the season. Cobb stole what was for 47 years a modern-record 96 bases, and the team's 100 wins proved to be the highest total in their first 33 years. But after running neck and neck with the Red Sox through most of August, the Tigers slumped a bit in early September—just enough for the Sox to take the flag by 2 ½ games. A close third-place finish the next year marked the Tigers' last serious challenge for 18 years.

In 1934, after six straight years in the second division, and only three years after their most distant finish ever (47 games out), the Tigers turned themselves around to win the pennant with a 101-53 record and a .656 winning percentage, the highest in club history. Two newly acquired veterans—manager/catcher Mickey Cochrane and outfielder Goose Goslin—enjoyed fine seasons at the bat, as did first baseman Hank Greenberg (.339, 139 RBIs) in his first full season, and second baseman Charlie Gehringer (.356, 127 RBIs). The two other infielders, third baseman Marv Owen and shortstop Billy Rogell enjoyed their finest seasons at the plate for a club whose batting average led the league at .300. It took the Tigers a month to get going, but by mid-July they had shot ahead of the Yankees, pulling away through August and September to win by seven games. But once again, victory in the World Series eluded them as the St. Louis Cardinals blew them away 11-0 in Game 7.

Paced by Greenberg's 170 RBIs in 1935, Detroit—after another slow start—shot up so sharply in July and August that even a September slump gave the Yankees no opportunity to catch them. And finally, in their fifth try, the Tigers won a world championship, overcoming Chicago in six games despite the loss of Greenberg, who broke his wrist in Game 2. Part-owner Frank Navin, who had run the club for three decades, had finally seen his Tigers reach the very top. A month later, after falling from a horse, he suffered a heart attack and died.

Del Baker had replaced Cochrane as manager when Detroit next made a run for the pennant in 1940. In a tight race the Tigers caught up with Cleveland in early September and traded the lead with them for two weeks before pulling ahead to stay with two wins in a three-game series. In the pennant clincher, Detroit's Floyd Giebell outdueled Cleveland great Bob Feller 2-0 for his third—and last—big league victory. In the World Series the Tigers lost once again, as Cincinnati came from behind in Game 7 for a 2-1 win.

Two losing seasons followed, and Steve O'Neill replaced Baker at the helm. In 1944, the wartime Tigers, behind the splendid pitching of workhorses Dizzy Trout and Hal Newhouser (one-two in ERA and innings pitched, and winners of 27 and 29 games), joined the race in late August and found themselves tied with the St. Louis Browns for first going into the last game of the season. But the Browns beat the Yankees and Detroit lost to Washington.

Hank Greenberg's release from military service in mid-1945 sparked another run for the pennant. They held the lead from mid-June through August, but in September a surging Washington caught up with them. The race once again went down to the final day, and the final inning, when Greenberg's grand slam overcame a St. Louis lead to give Detroit the flag over the idle Senators. Newhouser, with 25 wins and a 1.81 ERA, was named AL MVP for the second straight year. In the World Series his ERA shot up to 6.10, but he still managed to win two games (including the finale) as the Tigers took the Cubs in seven for their second world title.

In the 23 years that passed before their next pennant, the Tigers came close only twice. In 1950 they led the race through the middle of the season, but were caught by the Yankees late in August.

After retaking the lead in early September, the two clubs ran neck-and-neck for a while before Detroit fell away to second.

Two years later the Tigers reached their nadir: their first cellar finish. After a decade in which they finished no higher than fourth, they rebounded in 1961 as first baseman Norm Cash and left field-er Rocky Colavito both enjoyed the most explosive seasons of their careers. Compiling their best season record since 1934, Detroit led the league through parts of June and July. But this was the year of Maris and Mantle and 109 Yankee victories; when the season ended, the Tigers' 101 wins had earned them only second place.

They came much closer six years later in the great four-way race of 1967 that saw three clubs still contending on the final day, when the Tigers split a doubleheader to tie with Minnesota for second. If 1967 was a scramble, 1968 belonged to Detroit. Denny McLain won 31 games (the last major leaguer to win 30) to lead the team to a 103-win finish, 12 games ahead of Baltimore. Down three games to one in the World Series, the pitching of McLain in Game 6 and Mickey Lolich in Games 5 and 7 brought the Tigers back against the Cardinals and gave them their third world championship.

A strike at the start of 1972 contributed to the Tigers' first divisional title, which culminated a four-way race in the AL East. Detroit defeated Boston two games out of three at season's end, to edge the Sox by half a game. But if the strike had not wiped out an unequal number of games, the end of the season could have seen the two clubs tied.

The Tigers lost the pennant to Oakland with a 2-1 loss in the finale of a close Championship Series, and dropped out of contention for a decade. In 1974 they finished at the bottom of the division, and the next year lost 102 games. Detroit's highlight of the 1970s was the brief career of Mark "The Bird" Fidrych.

Finally, after seven seasons in the second division, Detroit put together a strong second half in strike-divided 1981, fading only at the end to tie for second. Three years later the Tigers were back on top with one of their best years. Opening the season 9-0, they ended April at 18-2, stretched their mark to 35-5 by late May, and were never headed, finishing a team-record 15 games in front, with 104 wins, their most ever. Their balanced pitching staff led the league in ERA, even though none of their starters finished among the top ten. Willie Hernandez (who with Aurelio Lopez compiled a 19-4 record from the bullpen, with 46 saves) earned both Cy Young and MVP awards. After sweeping Kansas City in the ALCS, the Tigers took the world championship—their fourth—from San Diego in five games.

In 1987 the Tigers caught the Blue Jays in the season's final series, tying them for the lead in the first game, moving to the front with a 12-inning win in the second game, and clinching the division crown in the finale, 1-0. In the ALCS, though, Minnesota stopped the favored Tigers, four games to one.

Injuries sidelined veteran keystoners Alan Trammell and Lou Whitaker more than a month each and derailed the season of starter Jeff Robinson in August just as he was emerging as ace of Detroit's pitchers. All the same, the Tigers led the AL East much of the 1988 season before falling back and rallied at season's end to finish second, one game behind the Boston Red Sox.

The next year, though, as new waves of injury broke over an aging lineup, the Tigers dropped into the division cellar in June and kept sinking, finishing with 103 losses and the worst record in the majors. But in 1990 Trammell rebounded from one of his worst seasons with one of his best and, with newly acquired first baseman Cecil Fielder, sparked a recovery to third place. Fielder, back in the AL after a season in Japan, topped the majors in home runs (with 51, the most in the AL since 1961), slugging percentage, and runs batted in.

The 1991 Tigers clawed their way back from an eight-game deficit in mid-July into a tie with first-place Toronto seven weeks later. But their grip wouldn't hold, and they finished tied for second with Boston. In 1992, for the third year in a row, Detroit led the AL in home runs, but this time their big bats couldn't lift the club above sixth place. Texas edged the Tigers for the home run crown in 1993, but Detroit challenged for their division lead through August and, after a dip in September, surged to tie Baltimore for third place. In strike-shortened 1994 they finished last in the AL East, 18 games out.

On the field in 1995 little of substance changed for the Tigers, as Fielder slammed 31 homers and the team finished a distant fourth (60-84), but momentous changes occurred off it. Sparky Anderson resigned as manager at season's end, and plans to replace Tiger Stadium with another downtown ballpark accelerated.

The Buddy Bell-led 1996 Tigers compiled baseball's worst

record (53-109). The season saw Cecil Fielder leave for the Yankees in midseason and Alan Trammell retire at season's end. The 1997 Tigers, however, were 26 games better than the previous season's club and paced by 100 RBIs from both first baseman Tony Clark and outfielder Bobby Higginson, the team finished third. The Tigers shifted to the AL Central in 1998 and the team foundered. Bell was dismissed late in the season and replaced by Larry Parrish. Detroit enjoyed a season-long celebration in the final year of Tiger Stadium in 1999, but the team stumbled home to a 69-92 record. After the Tiger Stadium finale, the Tigers replaced Parrish with Phil Garner. Two-time AL MVP Juan Gonzalez arrived from Texas for the inaugural season at Comerica Park.

Year-by-Year Finishes

MANAGER	YEAR	GAMES	FINISH (DIVISION)	
George Stallings	1901	74-61	.548	3	
Frank Dwyer	1902	52-83	.385	7	
Ed Barrow	1903	65-71	.478	5	
	1904	32-46	.410	7	7
Bobby Lowe	1904	30-44	.405	7	7
Bill Armour	1905	79-74	.516	3	
	1906	71-78	.477	6	
Hughie Jennings	1907	92-58	.613	1 ✔	
	1908	90-63	.588	1 ✔	
	1909	98-54	.645	1 ✔	
	1910	86-68	.558	3	
	1911	89-65	.578	2	
	1912	69-84	.451	6	
	1913	66-87	.431	6	
	1914	80-73	.523	4	
	1915	100-54	.649	2	
	1916	87-67	.565	3	
	1917	78-75	.510	4	
	1918	55-71	.437	7	
	1919	80-60	.571	4	
	1920	61-93	.396	7	

SYMBOL KEY

✪ Won World Series   ✔ Lost World Series   ⚲ Lost Division Series   ✖ Wild Card Champion

☛ Played regular season playoff game or series to determine wild card champion, division champion, or pennant winner   ◆ Tied

MANAGER	YEAR	GAMES	FINISH (DIVISION)			
Ty Cobb	1921	71-82	.464	6		
	1922	79-75	.513	3		
	1923	83-71	.539	2		
	1924	86-68	.558	3		
	1925	81-73	.526	4		
	1926	79-75	.513	6		
George Moriarty	1927	82-71	.536	4		
	1928	68-86	.442	6		
Bucky Harris	1929	70-84	.455	6		
	1930	75-79	.487	5		
	1931	61-93	.396	7		
	1932	76-75	.503	5		
	1933	73-79	.480	5	5	
Del Baker	1933	2-0	1.000	5	5	
Mickey Cochrane	1934	101-53	.656	1		
	1935	93-58	.616	1 ✪		
	1936	29-24	.547	3	2	
Del Baker	1936	18-16	.529	3	4	2
Mickey Cochrane	1936	36-31	.537	4	2	
	1937	16-13	.552	3	2	
Del Baker	1937	34-20	.630	3	3	2
Mickey Cochrane	1937	26-20	.565	3	2	2
Del Baker	1937	7-3	.700	2	2	2
Cy Perkins	1937	6-9	.400	2	2	
Mickey Cochrane	1938	47-51	.480	5	4	
Del Baker	1938	37-19	.661	5	4	
	1939	81-73	.526	5		
	1940	90-64	.584	1 ✔		
	1941	75-79	.487	4 ◆		
	1942	73-81	.474	5		

MANAGER	YEAR	GAMES	FINISH (DIVISION)			
Steve O'Neill	1943	78-76	.506	5		
	1944	88-66	.571	2		
	1945	88-65	.575	1 ✪		
	1946	92-62	.597	2		
	1947	85-69	.552	2		
	1948	78-76	.506	5		
Red Rolfe	1949	87-67	.565	4		
	1950	95-59	.617	2		
	1951	73-81	.474	5		
	1952	23-49	.319	8	8	
Fred Hutchinson	1952	27-55	.329	8	8	
	1953	60-94	.390	6		
	1954	68-86	.442	5		
Bucky Harris	1955	79-75	.513	5		
	1956	82-72	.532	5		
Jack Tighe	1957	78-76	.506	4		
	1958	21-28	.429	8	5	
Bill Norman	1958	56-49	.533	8	5	
	1959	2-15	.118	8	4	
Jimmy Dykes	1959	74-63	.540	8	4	
	1960	44-52	.458	6	6	
Billy Hitchcock	1960	1-0	1.000	6	6	6
Joe Gordon	1960	26-31	.456	6	6	
Bob Scheffing	1961	101-61	.623	2		
	1962	85-76	.528	4		
	1963	24-36	.400	9	5 ♦	
Chuck Dressen	1963	55-47	.539	9	5 ♦	
	1964	85-77	.525	4		
Bob Swift	1965	24-18	.571	3	4	
Chuck Dressen	1965	65-55	.542	3	4	

MANAGER	YEAR	GAMES	FINISH (DIVISION)			
	1966	16-10	.615	3	3	
Bob Swift	1966	32-25	.561	3	2	3
Frank Skaff	1966	40-39	.506	2	3	
Mayo Smith	1967	91-71	.562	2 ♦		
	1968	103-59	.636	1 ✪		
	1969	90-72	.556	2E		
	1970	79-83	.488	4E		
Billy Martin	1971	91-71	.562	2E		
	1972	86-70	.551	1E		
	1973	71-63	.530	3E	3E	
Joe Schultz	1973	14-14	.500	3E	3E	
Ralph Houk	1974	72-90	.444	6E		
	1975	57-102	.358	6E		
	1976	74-87	.460	5E		
	1977	74-88	.457	4E		
	1978	86-76	.531	5E		
Les Moss	1979	27-26	.509	5E	5E	
Dick Tracewski	1979	2-0	1.000	5E	5E	5E
Sparky Anderson	1979	56-50	.528	5E	5E	
	1980	84-78	.519	5E		
	1981	31-26	.544	4E		
	1981	29-23	.558	2E ♦		
	1982	83-79	.512	4E		
	1983	92-70	.568	2E		
	1984	104-58	.642	1E ✪		
	1985	84-77	.522	3E		
	1986	87-75	.537	3E		
	1987	98-64	.605	1E		
	1988	88-74	.543	2E		
	1989	59-103	.364	7E		

MANAGER	YEAR	GAMES	FINISH (DIVISION)		
	1990	79-83	.488	3E	
	1991	84-78	.519	2E ♦	
	1992	75-87	.463	6E	
	1993	85-77	.525	3E ♦	
	1994	53-62	.461	5E	
	1995	60-84	.417	4E	
Buddy Bell	1996	53-109	.327	5E	
	1997	79-83	.488	3E	
	1998	52-85	.380	5C	5C
Larry Parrish	1998	13-12	.520	5C	5C
	1999	69-92	.429	3C	

Tigers Postseason Play

WORLD SERIES 1907

Chicago Cubs (NL) 4; Detroit Tigers (AL) 0

Game 1 at Chi Oct 8 Chi 3-10-5, Det 3-9-3 (tie); Game 2 at Chi Oct 9 Chi 3-9-1, Det 1-9-1; Game 3 at Chi Oct 10 Chi 5-10-1, Det 1-6-1; Game 4 at Det Oct 11 Chi 6-7-2, Det 1-5-2; Game 5 at Det Oct 12 Chi 2-7-1, Det 0-7-2

The two-run lead that Detroit took into the bottom of the ninth inning of Game 1 proved to be its biggest of the Series. And it was short-lived, as Chicago—after Frank Chance's leadoff single—took advantage of a hit batsman, a fumble at third base, and a dropped third strike to even the score. Three scoreless extra innings later, darkness ended the game in a 3-3 tie.

The Tigers pitched well enough in the Series. Wild Bill Donovan and George Mullin, who provided more than 80 percent of Detroit's pitching, allowed only four earned runs each for a combined 1.89 ERA. But Cub pitchers gave up only four earned runs as a team, suffocating the Tigers with a team ERA of 0.75. And while Tiger fielders made one less error than the Cubs, their misplays proved more costly, permitting eight unearned runs to the Cubs' two.

Detroit's three-run eighth in the opener provided half of their Series scoring. Nine Tiger hits in Game 2 produced only one run, while the Cubs bunched six of their nine hits into two innings for three runs and the Series' first win. In Games 3 and 4, while the Tigers were twice again limited to a single run, the Cubs increased their run production to five and six, clustering 40 percent of their hits into two three-run innings, one in each game. Mordecai "Three Finger" Brown wrapped up the Series for Chicago with a shutout, as his Cubs blended a hit in each of the first two innings with three stolen bases and a Tiger error for the game's only two runs.

Detroit's 20-year-old Ty Cobb, the American League batting, RBI, and stolen base leader in his first full big league season, hit an anemic .200 in the World Series, stealing no bases and driving in no runs. If there were an offensive hero, it was Cub centerfielder Jimmy Slagle. At age 34, nearing the end of a 10-year major league career, he led both clubs with four RBIs and six stolen bases.

WORLD SERIES 1908
Chicago Cubs (NL) 4; Detroit Tigers (AL) 1

Game 1 at Det Oct 10 Chi 10-14-2, Det 6-10-4; Game 2 at Chi Oct 11 Chi 6-7-1, Det 1-4-1; Game 3 at Chi Oct 12 Det 8-11-4, Chi 3-7-2; Game 4 at Det Oct 13 Chi 3-10-0, Det 0-4-1; Game 5 at Det Oct 14 Chi 2-10-0, Det 0-3-0

The Tigers won their final game of the season to take their second straight pennant, and the Cubs won their third pennant in a row by defeating the Giants in a replay of an earlier tie. Ty Cobb and Detroit improved on their 1907 Series performance, as Cobb led his club in batting, hits, and RBIs, and the Tigers won a game. But the Cubs as a team hit 90 percentage points higher than Detroit, and outscored them 24-15, to take the Series with relative ease.

In Game 1, the Tigers took advantage of the Cubs' ragged fielding to score two runs in the eighth for a 6-5 lead. But in the top of the ninth, the Cubs erupted for five runs on six consecutive singles and a double steal, to win the game. The next day Chicago's Orval Overall held Detroit to four hits and one ninth-inning run. The Tigers' Wild Bill Donovan pitched even better for seven innings, holding Pittsburgh to a single in the sixth. But in the eighth, Joe Tinker's two-run homer—the first in a World Series since 1903—began an assault that ended only after six Cubs had crossed the plate.

Detroit finally manufactured a Series win, pummeling Jack Pfiester in Game 3 for 10 hits (six of them in the sixth inning) and an 8-3 victory. But that was their last burst. As the Series moved to Detroit for Games 4 and 5, the Tiger offense collapsed. Three Finger Brown, the winner as a reliever in Game One, won Game 4 as a starter, shutting out the Tigers on four hits. The Cubs needed only three of their 10 hits, combining them with a couple of walks and stolen bases, and a muffed fly ball, to score twice in the third inning and once in the ninth.

Only 6,210 spectators—the smallest World Series crowd of the Century—saw Overall strike out four Tigers in the first inning of Game 5 (one reached first on a wild pitch) in what became a three-hit shutout. Meanwhile, his Cubs unloaded for 10 hits, defeating Donovan a second time, scoring runs in the first and fifth innings. Overall—after yielding a leadoff walk to Cobb in the fifth— retired Cobb on a force play and set down the final 11 men to face him.

WORLD SERIES 1909

Pittsburgh Pirates (NL) 4; Detroit Tigers (AL) 3

Game 1 at Pit Oct 8 Pit 4-5-0, Det 1-6-4; Game 2 at Pit Oct 9 Det 7-9-3,
Pit 2-5-1; Game 3 at Det Oct 11 Pit 8-10-3, Det 6-10-5; Game 4 at Det Oct 12
Det 5-8-0, Pit 0-5-6; Game 5 at Pit Oct 13 Pit 8-10-2, Det 4-6-1; Game 6 at Det
Oct 14 Det 5-10-3, Pit 4-7-3; Game 7 at Det Oct 16 Pit 8-7-0, Det 0-6-3

Babe Adams, a 27-year-old rookie pitcher, was only the fifth biggest
winner on the Pittsburgh staff. But his fine 12-3 record was supported
by a team-best 1.11 ERA, and manager Fred Clarke started him in the
Series opener against Detroit's ace George Mullin (who had led the
American League with a career-high 29 wins). Mullin pitched well,
giving up only one earned run—manager/outfielder Clarke's homer in
the fourth inning. But four Tiger errors led to three Pirate runs in the
fifth and sixth. Meanwhile, Adams, after yielding a run in the first,
pitched shutout ball the rest of the way for the win.

Detroit came back in Game 2 with seven runs (including Ty
Cobb's theft of home) as Wild Bill Donovan held the Pirates to two
runs on five hits. In Game 3 the Pirates took an early lead, which
Detroit, despite rallies in the seventh and ninth innings, was unable to
overcome. Errors determined most of the scoring, as only one of
Detroit's six runs and two of Pittsburgh's eight were earned.

Mullin shut out the Pirates on five hits in Game 4, striking out 10
men as Detroit scored five runs (all earned, despite Pittsburgh's six
errors) to drive out starter Lefty Leifield after four innings. The seesaw
Series continued in Game 5, with Babe Adams winning his second
game behind his Pirates' ten-hit, eight-run attack. Adams gave up lead-

off homers to Davy Jones in the first and Sam Crawford in the eighth. But Pittsburgh's Clarke more than countered these with his three-run shot in the seventh. (All three homers were hit into temporary seats in center field.)

Back in Detroit for Game 6, the Tigers evened the Series for the third time, Mullin winning his second game in a close contest that saw Pittsburgh pull within a run of tying the game in the ninth before a runner thrown out at home and a game-ending double play cut their rally dead.

In the finale it was Babe Adams once again, scattering six Tiger hits for an easy 8-0 win, his third of the Series. Detroit had done better than ever, but still lost its third World Series in three consecutive attempts. A quarter century would pass before they would have a chance to try again.

WORLD SERIES 1934

St.Louis Cardinals (NL) 4; Detroit Tigers (AL) 3

Game 1 at Det Oct 3 StL 8-13-2, Det 3-8-5; Game 2 at Det Oct 4 Det 3-7-0, StL 2-7-3; Game 3 at StL Oct 5 StL 4-9-1, Det 1-8-2; Game 4 at StL Oct 6 Det 10-13-1, StL 4-10-5; Game 5 at StL Oct 7 Det 3-7-0, StL 1-7-1; Game 6 at Det Oct 8 StL 4-10-2, Det 3-7-1; Game 7 at Det Oct 9 StL 11-17-1, Det 0-6-3

Pitching brothers Dizzy and Paul Dean won seven games in 10 days to give the Cardinals the pennant on the final day of the season. In the Series they continued their winning ways, chalking up all four Cardinal victories—as Dizzy predicted. Dizzy pitched the opener in Detroit. Given a 3-0 lead, thanks to five Tiger errors in the first three innings, he breezed to an 8-3 win.

Detroit's Schoolboy Rowe brought the Tigers back with a pitching masterpiece in Game 2. After giving up single runs in the second and third innings, he allowed only one runner to reach base over the next nine as his Tigers tied the score in the ninth, and won it on two walks and a single in the 12th.

Paul Dean nearly pitched a shutout in Game 3, yielding a harmless run with two out in the ninth after the Cards had built him a 4-0 lead. Brother Diz figured in a curious and painful play in Game 4. Pinch-running in the fourth inning, he was beaned by a would-be double-play throw as he ran to second. The tying run scored from third on the play, but Detroit's pitcher Eldon Auker shut out the Cards through the final five innings, and his teammates scored six more runs to bury St. Louis, 10-4, evening the Series at two apiece. Diz was rushed to the hospital, but as no damage was found he started Game 5 the next day. He pitched well enough, but Detroit's Tommy Bridges pitched better, giving the Cardinals only one run to the Tigers' three.

Paul Dean evened the Series again with a win against Rowe in a closely contested sixth game. A grounder through Dean's legs allowed the Tigers to tie the game in the sixth inning, but Paul redeemed his error in the seventh when he singled in the tie-breaking—and as it turned out, winning—run. Dizzy came back after only a day's rest to hurl a six-hit shutout in the finale. He also scored the game's first run and drove in the sixth with a double and single in his team's seven-run third. Three innings later, frustrated Tiger fans, angered by Cardinal Joe Medwick's rough slide into their third baseman, pelted Medwick with food and bottles, halting the game for 20 minutes until Commissioner Landis ordered Medwick from the game. The delay only forestalled Detroit's defeat, as the Cards took the title game 11-0.

WORLD SERIES 1935

Detroit Tigers (AL) 4; Chicago Cubs (NL) 2

Game 1 at Det Oct 2 Chi 3-7-0, Det 0-4-3; Game 2 at Det Oct 3 Det 8-9-2, Chi 3-6-1; Game 3 at Chi Oct 4 Det 6-12-2, Chi 5-10-3; Game 4 at Chi Oct 5 Det 2-7-0, Chi 1-5-2; Game 5 at Chi Oct 6 Chi 3-8-0, Det 1-7-1; Game 6 at Det Oct 7 Det 4-12-1, Chi 3-12-0

With a 21-game September winning streak, the Cubs vaulted over the Giants and Cardinals to face Detroit in the Series, and for a moment it seemed as if their momentum might carry them past the Tigers as well. Chicago scored two runs off Schoolboy Rowe in the top of the first in the opener, and right fielder Frank Demaree homered to open the ninth as Lon Warneke blanked the Tigers on four hits. But Detroit retaliated quickly in Game 2, driving out starter Charlie Root in the first inning with four runs (including Hank Greenberg's two-run homer) before Root had had a chance to record even one out. Tiger pitcher Rocky Bridges gained an easy 8-3 win, but Greenberg broke a wrist and was finished for the Series.

In Game 3 the Cubs scored three times before Detroit countered with their first run in the sixth. But a walk and four Tiger hits in the eighth put the Bengals ahead, 4-3. Billy Rogell's baserunning, as he turned a foiled steal into a rundown, permitted a fifth Tiger to cross the plate. Two Cub runs in the last of the ninth tied the score, but Detroit pulled out the victory in the 11th as a pair of singles sandwiched Fred Lindstrom's error at third to give them an unearned run.

Detroit's Alvin "General" Crowder followed up the Tigers' advantage the next day with a neat five-hit 2-1 win. Once again the Cubs bobbled away the game, this time with two sixth-inning errors that enabled Detroit to score the winning run without a hit. Chuck Klein's two-run homer saved Chicago from elimination in Game Five as Lon Warneke and Bill Lee shut out the Tigers through eight before letting in a harmless run in the ninth.

Chicago's Larry French and Tiger Rocky Bridges yielded 12 hits apiece in Game 6. Cub second baseman Billy Herman singled in a run in the third to tie the score, and homered for two more runs in the fifth to put the Cubs ahead. But the Tigers tied it up an inning later, and took their first world title ever when Goose Goslin singled in Mickey Cochrane with two out in the bottom of the ninth.

WORLD SERIES 1940

Cincinnati Reds (NL) 4; Detroit Tigers (AL) 3

Game 1 at Cin Oct 2 Det 7-10-1, Cin 2-8-3; Game 2 at Cin Oct 3 Cin 5-9-0, Det 3-3-1; Game 3 at Det Oct 4 Det 7-13-1, Cin 4-10-1; Game 4 at Det Oct 5 Cin 5-11-1, Det 2-5-1; Game 5 at Det Oct 6 Det 8-13-0, Cin 0-3-0; Game 6 at Cin Oct 7 Cin 4-10-2, Det 0-5-0; Game 7 at Cin Oct 8 Cin 2-7-1, Det 1-7-0

The Tigers outpitched and outslugged the Reds, and scored six more runs than the Reds did. What they failed to do was win the Series.

Tiger ace Bobo Newsom, who had enjoyed what would be his finest season in a long career, carried his mastery into the Series opener. Detroit gave him an early lead, driving out Red starter Paul Derringer with five runs in the second inning, and added a pair of runs in the fifth on Bruce Campbell's home run. Newsom, meanwhile, held the Reds to single runs in the fourth and eighth.

Cincinnati's Bucky Walters walked the first two Tigers he faced in Game 2, and both scored. But two Red runs in the second tied the game, Jimmy Ripple's two-run homer an inning later gave them the lead, and pitcher Walters scored an insurance run in the fourth after doubling. Another Tiger walk in the sixth led to their third run, but Walters retired the remaining Tigers in order.

The Series moved to Detroit and the lead to the Tigers in Game 3. Detroit's Rocky Bridges yielded ten hits and four runs, but his team-mates responded with 13 hits and seven runs, including a pair of two-run homers by Rudy York and Pinky Higgins in the seventh. Cincinnati again evened the Series the next day, though, with five runs to support Derringer's five-hit, two-run pitching. Although Newsom's father had suffered a fatal heart attack the day after seeing his son win the opener, the son pitched Game 5, and improved on his previous performance with a three-hit shutout. Hank Greenberg's homer in the third inning accounted for the first three of the Tigers' eight runs in their lopsided win.

The Reds returned home needing to win the final two games. Like Newsom, Bucky Walters bettered his earlier win with a shutout in Game Six, and drove in two of the Reds' four runs, one with a solo homer in the eighth. In the Series finale, Newsom and Derringer found themselves evenly matched. The Tigers scored a run in the third, while

Newsom held Cincinnati scoreless through six. But in the seventh, leadoff doubles by Frank McCormick and Jimmy Ripple, plus a successful bunt and a fly to deep center, gave the Reds two runs—all they needed as Derringer stopped the Tigers through the final six innings for the victory.

WORLD SERIES 1945

Detroit Tigers (AL) 4; Chicago Cubs (NL) 3

Game 1 at Det Oct 3 Chi 9-13-0, Det 0-6-0; Game 2 at Det Oct 4 Det 4-7-0, Chi 1-7-0; Game 3 at Det Oct 5 Chi 3-8-0, Det 0-1-2; Game 4 at Chi Oct 6 Det 4-7-1, Chi 1-5-1; Game 5 at Chi Oct 7 Det 8-11-0, Chi 4-7-2; Game 6 at Chi Oct 8 Chi 8-15-3, Det 7-13-1; Game 7 at Chi Oct 10 Det 9-9-1, Chi 3-10-0

As World War II ended during the summer, military major leaguers beganreturning to their clubs. Hank Greenberg's return in July provided the spark needed for Detroit's narrow pennant victory, and his three-run homer in Game 2 of the World Series proved to be the decisive blow in the Tigers' successful struggle for the world title.

Chicago started strong as Cub ace Hank Borowy shut out the Tigers on six singles while his teammates drove out Tiger ace Hal Newhouser with seven runs in the first three innings, to win 9-0. Chicago continued its assault the next day with a run in the top of the fourth, but in the fifth inning Tiger Doc Cramer—with two out and two on—singled in the tying run, and Greenberg followed with his tie-breaking homer for three additional runs. Detroit pitcher Virgil Trucks (who had returned from the navy in time to pitch in the regular-season finale) held the Cubs scoreless after the fourth inning to gain the victory and even the Series.

Chicago's Claude Passeau moved the Cubs back into the Series lead with a one-hit shutout in Game 3, but Tiger Dizzy Trout's five-hitter in Game 4 again evened the Series. The Tigers bunched four of their seven hits in the fourth inning for all four of their runs.

Detroit took the Series lead for the first time with an 8-4 win in Game 5. Borowy and Newhouser faced each other as they had in the opener, but this time Borowy was hit hard. Driven out when four Tigers opened the sixth inning with safe hits, he took the loss as Newhouser went the distance for the win.

In Game 6, Chicago concluded the seventh inning of a heavy-hitting game leading 7-3. Detroit tied the score with four runs in the top of the eighth (capped by Greenberg's home run), but in the last of the twelfth the Cubs' Stan Hack doubled home the winning run.

Two days later in the finale, Cub manager Charlie Grimm started Borowy, who had relieved for four shutout innings to win Game 6. But this third appearance in four days proved too much. Removed after the first three batters to face him singled, he took the loss, as the Tigers went on to score nine runs to the Cubs' three.

WORLD SERIES 1968

Detroit Tigers (AL) 4; St.Louis Cardinals (NL) 3

Game 1 at StL Oct 2 StL 4-6-0, Det 0-5-3; Game 2 at StL Oct 3 Det 8-13-1, StL 1-6-1; Game 3 at Det Oct 5 StL 7-13-0, Det 3-4-0; Game 4 at Det Oct 6 StL 10-13-0, Det 1-5-4; Game 5 at Det Oct 7 Det 5-9-1, StL 3-9-0; Game 6 at StL Oct 9 Det 13-12-1, StL 1-9-1; Game 7 at StL Oct 10 Det 4-8-1, StL 1-5-0

In this "year of the pitcher," Tiger Denny McLain's 31 wins were the most for a major leaguer in 37 years. Cardinal Bob Gibson's 1.12 ERA was the majors' best since Dutch Leonard's 1.01 in 1914, and his 13 season shutouts tied for third best of all time. In the Series, though, it was Detroit's second-best pitcher—Mickey Lolich—who emerged as the hero.

McLain came off second-best against Gibson in the opener. He yielded only three hits in his five innings, but two Cardinal singles in the fourth combined with a pair of walks and a Tiger error for three runs. Gibson, meanwhile, was in the process of striking out a Series-record 17 batters on the way to a five-hit shutout. But Lolich brought Detroit back in Game 2. He struck out nine, and his third-inning home run (the only one of his major league career) for the second Tiger run provided all the scoring needed for a Detroit victory, although the Tigers kept putting runs across for an eventual 8-1 win.

Home runs accounted for most of the scoring in Game 3. Veteran Al Kaline's two-run shot in the third opened the scoring, but Cardinal Tim McCarver's three-run blast in the fifth put St. Louis ahead. Tiger Dick McAuliffe's solo shot later in the inning brought Detroit within one run of a tie, but the Cardinals put the game away on Orlando Cepeda's three-run homer in the seventh.

McLain faced Gibson again in Game 4, and again came off second-best. Cardinal Lou Brock led off the game with a home run, and before the end of the third inning McLain was gone. Gibson gave up a solo homer to Tiger Jim Northrup in the fourth, but that was the only Detroit run he allowed. Gibson homered himself and struck out 10 in an easy 10-1 win.

Down three games to one, the Tigers were saved from elimination by Lolich's arm. Although three Cardinal hits in the top of the first (including Orlando Cepeda's second homer of the Series) gave St. Louis a quick three runs, Lolich held the Cards scoreless the rest of the game as his Tigers fought back with two runs in the fourth and three more in the seventh (with a rally started by Lolich's single). McLain finally came through in Game 6, evening the Series with an easy 13-1 victory, in which Jim Northrup's grand slam provided the big blow of a 10-run third inning.

Lolich and Gibson—both 2-0 in the Series—faced off in the finale. Gibson broke his own World Series strikeout record in the third inning (finishing with eight for the game and 35 for the Series), and both pitchers hurled shutout ball through six innings. But four two-out Tiger hits in the top of the seventh—including a misplayed fly ball in center field—put three runs on the board, and another run in the ninth made the score 4-0. In the last of the ninth, Mike Shannon's solo homer spoiled Lolich's shutout, but not his third Series win—or the Tigers' comeback world title.

CHAMPIONSHIP SERIES 1972

Oakland A's 3; Detroit Tigers 2

Game 1 at Oak Oct 7 Oak 3-10-1, Det 2-6-2; Game 2 at Oak Oct 8 Oak 5-8-0, Det 0-3-1; Game 3 at Det Oct 10 Det 3-8-1, Oak 0-7-0; Game 4 at Det Oct 11 Det 4-10-1, Oak 3-9-2; Game 5 at Det Oct 12 Oak 2-4-0, Det 1-5-2

Oakland turned back the Tigers in the first two games, but Detroit evened the series before succumbing in the fifth game.

In Game 1, Tiger Al Kaline homered off Rollie Fingers in the 11th to give starter Mickey Lolich a 2-1 lead. But in the last of the inning, pinch hitter Gonzalo Marquez singled off Tiger reliever Chuck Seelbach with two on to drive in the tying run, and Gene Tenace scored to win it on the same play as right fielder Kaline threw the ball away. Blue Moon Odom increased the A's series lead with a three-hit shutout in Game 2, but Detroit's Joe Coleman retaliated with 14 strikeouts and a shutout of his own to save the Tigers from elimination in Game Three.

In Game 4 the A's pulled out of a 1-1 tie with two runs in the top of the 10th. But Detroit in its half of the inning went through three Oakland relievers for three runs and the win. In the finale, after Odom, the A's starter, had given Detroit a run and a brief lead in the first, he and Vida Blue divided eight shutout innings between them as the A's scored twice to capture their first pennant since Connie Mack won his last in Philadelphia forty-one years earlier.

CHAMPIONSHIP SERIES 1984
Detroit Tigers 3; Kansas City Royals 0
Game 1 at KC Oct 2 Det 8-14-0, KC 1-5-1; Game 2 at KC Oct 3 Det 5-8-1, KC 3-10-3; Game 3 at Det Oct 5 Det 1-3-0, KC 0-3-3
The heavily favored Tigers swept the series, but not without difficulty, despite a 14-hit, three-homer, 8-1 romp in the opener.

Games 2 and 3 were much tighter. In the second game, after

Detroit had built a 3-0 lead over the first three innings, Royal rookie starter Bret Saberhagen settled down and blanked the Tigers for the next five innings as K.C. inched its way to a tie with runs in the fourth, seventh, and eighth. Through the ninth and 10th innings, Tiger reliever Aurelio Lopez and Royal Dan Quisenberry dueled scorelessly, but in the top of the eleventh Johnny Grubb doubled home two Tiger runs. Lopez struggled but held the Royals scoreless in the last of the 11th for the win.

In Game 3, the Royals' Charlie Leibrandt and Tigers' Milt Wilcox and Willie Hernandez hurled matching three-hitters. But the Tigers secured the game—and the pennant—when Chet Lemon scored on a broken double play in the second inning for the game's only run.

WORLD SERIES 1984

Detroit Tigers (AL) 4; San Diego Padres (NL) 1

Game 1 at SD Oct 9 Det 3-8-0, SD 2-8-1; Game 2 at SD Oct 10 SD 5-11-0,
Det 3-7-3; Game 3 at Det Oct 12 Det 5-7-0, SD 2-5-0; Game 4 at Det Oct 13
Det 4-7-0, SD 2-10-2; Game 5 at Det Oct 14 Det 8-11-1, SD 4-10-1

Few objective observers expected the Padres (playing in their first World Series) to best the mighty Tigers—and they didn't. Detroit's first two batters in Game 1 hit safely to produce the Series' first scoring before an out had been recorded. San Diego countered with three two-out hits in their half of the first to go ahead 2-1. But Detroit starter Jack Morris settled down to shut out the Padres over the final eight innings, and his Tigers scored the tying and winning runs in the fifth on Larry Herndon's two-run homer. The Tigers scored again in Game 2 before the first out was recorded and drove out Padre starter Ed Whitson with three first-inning runs on five singles. But this time Detroit was shut out over the final eight, while San Diego scored single runs in the first and fourth and the winning runs in the fifth on a three-run homer by the normally light-hitting Kurt Bevacqua.

The Tigers won Game 3 on walks—a Series-record 11—as the Series moved to Detroit. After scoring their first two runs in the second on a single and Marty Castillo's home run, they continued on to put across two more in the inning on a pair of hits alternated with three walks (the last with the bases full). Three more walks an inning later, followed by a hit batsman, gave Detroit its final run in what became a 5-2 win.

Alan Trammell's two-run homer in the first inning of Game 4 put the Tigers ahead to stay. Tiger pitcher Jack Morris gave up a solo home run to Terry Kennedy in the second, but Trammell swatted a second two-run shot an inning later for a 4-1 lead. Morris let a second Padre runner score on a wild pitch in the ninth, but then retired Kennedy for the third out and his second Series win. Kirk Gibson's two home runs framed Tiger scoring in the final game. His two-run shot in the first inning opened the game's scoring. San Diego tied it up with runs in the third and fourth, but Detroit took a 5-3 lead with runs in the fifth and seventh.

Bevacqua brought the Padres within a run of tying the game with his second Series homer in the eighth, but Gibson ended the Padre hopes with a three-run blast half an inning later.

CHAMPIONSHIP SERIES 1987

Minnesota Twins 4; Detroit Tigers 1

Game 1 at Min Oct 7 Min 8-10-0, Det 5-10-0; Game 2 at Min Oct 8 Min 6-6-0, Det 3-7-1; Game 3 at Det Oct 10 Det 7-7-0, Min 6-8-1; Game 4 at Det Oct 11 Min 5-7-1, Det 3-7-3; Game 5 at Det Oct 12 Min 9-15-1, Det 5-9-1

The Tigers, with the best overall won-lost record in the majors, were favored to defeat the ninth-ranked Twins, although Minnesota held the home field advantage and the major leagues' best record at home. Tiger pitcher Doyle Alexander—he had been 9-0 since joining Detroit in mid-August—took a 5-4 lead into the last of the eighth in Game 1. But a single and double drove him out, and before the inning was over three more Twins had scored to sew up their first win. Detroit scored twice in the second inning the next day, but the Twins responded later in the inning with three runs, two on Tim Laudner's double off Tiger ace Jack Morris, and increased their lead in the fourth and fifth to seal Morris' first loss in Minnesota after 11 wins.

The Tigers won a game after the series moved to Detroit, when Pat Sheridan's two-run homer in the eighth inning of Game 3 restored a lead they had squandered in the middle innings. But that was it for Detroit, as the Twins surprised everyone by subduing the Tigers in their den. In Game 4 they took the lead for good on Greg Gagne's fourth-inning home run. And in Game 5, after initiating the scoring with four runs in the second, Minnesota pushed on to a 9-5 win and their first pennant in twenty-two years.

Team Records

Active players in ALL CAPS

CAREER

GAMES

2834	Al Kaline, 1953-1974
2806	Ty Cobb, 1905-1926
2390	Lou Whitaker, 1977-1995
2323	Charlie Gehringer, 1924-1942
2293	Alan Trammell, 1977-1996

RUNS

2088	Ty Cobb, 1905-1926
1774	Charlie Gehringer, 1924-1942
1622	Al Kaline, 1953-1974
1386	Lou Whitaker, 1977-1995
1242	Donie Bush, 1908-1921

HITS

3900	Ty Cobb, 1905-1926
3007	Al Kaline, 1953-1974
2839	Charlie Gehringer, 1924-1942
2499	Harry Heilmann, 1914-1929
2466	Sam Crawford, 1903-1917

DOUBLES

665	Ty Cobb, 1905-1926
574	Charlie Gehringer, 1924-1942
498	Al Kaline, 1953-1974
497	Harry Heilmann, 1914-1929
420	Lou Whitaker, 1977-1995

TRIPLES

284	Ty Cobb, 1905-1926
249	Sam Crawford, 1903-1917
146	Charlie Gehringer, 1924-1942
145	Harry Heilmann, 1914-1929
136	Bobby Veach, 1912-1923

HOME RUNS

399	Al Kaline, 1953-1974
373	Norm Cash, 1960-1974
306	Hank Greenberg, 1930-1946
262	Willie Horton, 1963-1977
245	Cecil Fielder, 1990-1996

RUNS BATTED IN

1805	Ty Cobb, 1905-1926
1583	Al Kaline, 1953-1974
1442	Harry Heilmann, 1914-1929
1427	Charlie Gehringer, 1924-1942
1264	Sam Crawford, 1903-1917

STOLEN BASES

865	Ty Cobb, 1905-1926
400	Donie Bush, 1908-1921
317	Sam Crawford, 1903-1917
294	Ron LeFlore, 1974-1979
236	Alan Trammell, 1977-1996

BASES ON BALLS

1277	Al Kaline, 1953-1974
1197	Lou Whitaker, 1977-1995
1186	Charlie Gehringer, 1924-1942
1148	Ty Cobb, 1905-1926
1125	Donie Bush, 1908-1921

BATTING AVERAGE

.368	Ty Cobb, 1905-1926
.342	Harry Heilmann, 1914-1929
.337	Bob Fothergill, 1922-1930
.325	George Kell, 1946-1952
.321	Heinie Manush, 1923-1927

ON-BASE PERCENTAGE

.434	Ty Cobb, 1905-1926
.420	Johnny Bassler, 1921-1927
.412	Hank Greenberg, 1930-1946
.412	Roy Cullenbine, 1938-1947
.410	Harry Heilmann, 1914-1929

SLUGGING AVERAGE

.616	Hank Greenberg, 1930-1946
.518	Harry Heilmann, 1914-1929
.516	Ty Cobb, 1905-1926
.503	TONY CLARK, 1995-1999
.503	Rudy York, 1934-1945

GAMES PITCHED

545	John Hiller, 1965-1980
538	Hooks Dauss, 1912-1926
508	Mickey Lolich, 1963-1975
493	Dizzy Trout, 1939-1952
491	Mike Henneman, 1987-1995

GAMES STARTED

459	Mickey Lolich, 1963-1975
408	Jack Morris, 1977-1990
395	George Mullin, 1902-1913
388	Hooks Dauss, 1912-1926
373	Hal Newhouser, 1939-1953

COMPLETE GAMES

336	George Mullin, 1902-1913
245	Hooks Dauss, 1912-1926
213	Bill Donovan, 1903-1918
212	Hal Newhouser, 1939-1953
200	Tommy Bridges, 1930-1946

SAVES

154	Mike Henneman, 1987-1995
125	John Hiller, 1965-1980
120	Willie Hernandez, 1984-1989
89	TODD JONES, 1997-1999
85	Aurelio Lopez, 1979-1985

SHUTOUTS

39	Mickey Lolich, 1963-1975
34	George Mullin, 1902-1913
33	Tommy Bridges, 1930-1946
33	Hal Newhouser, 1939-1953
29	Bill Donovan, 1903-1918

WINS

223	Hooks Dauss, 1912-1926
209	George Mullin, 1902-1913
207	Mickey Lolich, 1963-1975
200	Hal Newhouser, 1939-1953
198	Jack Morris, 1977-1990

STRIKEOUTS

2679	Mickey Lolich, 1963-1975
1980	Jack Morris, 1977-1990
1770	Hal Newhouser, 1939-1953
1674	Tommy Bridges, 1930-1946
1406	Jim Bunning, 1955-1963

WON-LOST PERCENTAGE

.654	Denny McLain, 1963-1970
.639	Aurelio Lopez, 1979-1985
.629	Schoolboy Rowe, 1933-1942
.626	Mike Henneman, 1987-1995
.616	Harry Coveleski, 1914-1918

EARNED RUN AVERAGE

2.34	Harry Coveleski, 1914-1918
2.38	Ed Killian, 1904-1910
2.42	Ed Summers, 1908-1912
2.49	Bill Donovan, 1903-1918
2.61	Ed Siever, 1901-1908

SEASON

RUNS

147	Ty Cobb, 1911
144	Ty Cobb, 1915
144	Charlie Gehringer, 1930
144	Charlie Gehringer, 1936
144	Hank Greenberg, 1938

HITS

248	Ty Cobb, 1911
237	Harry Heilmann, 1921
227	Charlie Gehringer, 1936
226	Ty Cobb, 1912
225	Ty Cobb, 1917
225	Harry Heilmann, 1925

DOUBLES

63	Hank Greenberg, 1934
60	Charlie Gehringer, 1936
56	George Kell, 1950
55	Gee Walker, 1936
50	Charlie Gehringer, 1934
50	Hank Greenberg, 1940
50	Harry Heilmann, 1927

TRIPLES

26	Sam Crawford, 1914
25	Sam Crawford, 1903
24	Ty Cobb, 1911
24	Ty Cobb, 1917

| 23 | Ty Cobb, 1912 |
| 23 | Sam Crawford, 1913 |

HOME RUNS

58	Hank Greenberg, 1938
51	Cecil Fielder, 1990
45	Rocky Colavito, 1961
44	Cecil Fielder, 1991
44	Hank Greenberg, 1946

RUNS BATTED IN

183	Hank Greenberg, 1937
170	Hank Greenberg, 1935
150	Hank Greenberg, 1940
146	Hank Greenberg, 1938
140	Rocky Colavito, 1961

STOLEN BASES

96	Ty Cobb, 1915
83	Ty Cobb, 1911
78	Ron LeFlore, 1979
76	Ty Cobb, 1909
74	BRIAN HUNTER, 1997

BASES ON BALLS

137	Roy Cullenbine, 1947
135	Eddie Yost, 1959
132	TONY PHILLIPS, 1993
125	Eddie Yost, 1960
124	Norm Cash, 1961

BATTING AVERAGE

.420	Ty Cobb, 1911
.409	Ty Cobb, 1912
.403	Harry Heilmann, 1923
.401	Ty Cobb, 1922
.398	Harry Heilmann, 1927

ON-BASE PERCENTAGE

.487	Norm Cash, 1961
.486	Ty Cobb, 1915
.481	Harry Heilmann, 1923
.475	Harry Heilmann, 1927
.468	Ty Cobb, 1925

SLUGGING AVERAGE

.683	Hank Greenberg, 1938
.670	Hank Greenberg, 1940
.668	Hank Greenberg, 1937
.662	Norm Cash, 1961
.632	Harry Heilmann, 1923

GAMES

88	MIKE MYERS, 1997
88	SEAN RUNYAN, 1998
83	MIKE MYERS, 1996
80	Willie Hernandez, 1984
74	Willie Hernandez, 1985

GAMES STARTED

45	Mickey Lolich, 1971
44	George Mullin, 1904
42	Mickey Lolich, 1973

42	George Mullin, 1907
41	Joe Coleman, 1974
41	Mickey Lolich, 1972
41	Mickey Lolich, 1974
41	Denny McLain, 1968
41	Denny McLain, 1969
41	George Mullin, 1905

COMPLETE GAMES

42	George Mullin, 1904
35	Roscoe Miller, 1901
35	George Mullin, 1905
35	George Mullin, 1906
35	George Mullin, 1907

SAVES

38	John Hiller, 1973
32	Willie Hernandez, 1984
31	Willie Hernandez, 1985
31	TODD JONES, 1997
30	TODD JONES, 1999

SHUTOUTS

9	Denny McLain, 1969
8	Ed Killian, 1905
8	Hal Newhouser, 1945
7	Billy Hoeft, 1955
7	George Mullin, 1904
7	Dizzy Trout, 1944

WINS

31	Denny McLain, 1968
29	George Mullin, 1909
29	Hal Newhouser, 1944
27	Dizzy Trout, 1944
26	Hal Newhouser, 1946

STRIKEOUTS

308	Mickey Lolich, 1971
280	Denny McLain, 1968
275	Hal Newhouser, 1946
271	Mickey Lolich, 1969
250	Mickey Lolich, 1972

WON-LOST PERCENTAGE

.862	Bill Donovan, 1907
.842	Schoolboy Rowe, 1940
.838	Denny McLain, 1968
.808	Bobo Newsom, 1940
.784	George Mullin, 1909

EARNED RUN AVERAGE

1.64	Ed Summers, 1908
1.71	Ed Killian, 1909
1.78	Ed Killian, 1907
1.81	Hal Newhouser, 1945
1.91	Ed Siever, 1902

MOST CONSECUTIVE GAMES
BATTING SAFELY

40	Ty Cobb, 1911
35	Ty Cobb, 1917
30	Goose Goslin, 1934
30	Ron LeFlore, 1976
29	Dale Alexander, 1930
29	Pete Fox, 1935

MOST CONSECUTIVE SCORELESS
INNINGS

33	Harry Coveleskie, 1914

NO-HIT GAMES

George Mullin

Det vs StL AL, 7-0; July 4, 1912
(2nd game).

Virgil Trucks

Det vs Was AL, 1-0; May 15, 1952.

Virgil Trucks

Det at NY AL, 1-0; August 25, 1952.

Jim Bunning

Det at Bos AL, 3-0; July 20, 1958
(1st game).

Jack Morris

Det at Chi AL, 4-0; April 7, 1984.

Tigers Ballparks

TIGER STADIUM

CAPACITY: 52,416

STYLE: Classic.

OCCUPANT: AL Tigers, April 20, 1912 to Sept. 27, 1999, NNL Stars 1920-31, NEWL Wolves 1932, NNL Stars 1933, NAL Stars 1937.

EVENT: 1941 All-Star Game, 1951 All-Star Game, 1971 All-Star Game.

A.K.A.: Bennett Park 1896 to 1911, Navin Field 1912 to 1937, Briggs Stadium 1938 to 1960.

SURFACE: Bluegrass.

DIMENSIONS: Left Field: 339-367; Left Center: 365; Center Field: 420-467; Right Center: 370-375; Right Field: 367-372 (1921-31), 302-325 (1936-99); Backstop: 54.35-66; Foul Territory: Small

FENCES: Left Field 20-30 (1935-37), 9-15 (1938-99); Center Field: 9-15; Right of Flag Pole: 7; Right Field: 8-30; Flag Pole: 125 in play (5 feet in front of fence in center field, just left of dead center)

PHENOMENA: First named for Frank Navin, Tigers president 1908-1935. Right field second deck overhangs the lower deck by 10 feet. Screen in right in 1944 and in 1961 required balls to be hit into the second deck to be home runs. Only doubledecked bleachers in the majors — upper deck from left-center to center, lower deck from center to right-center. There is a string of spotlights mounted under the overhang to illuminate the right field warning track which is shadowed from the normal light standards. When slugging teams came to visit, manager Ty Cobb had the groundskeepers put in temporary bleachers in the outfield, so that long drives would be just ground-rule doubles. Sign above entrance to visitors' clubhouse: "Visitors' Clubhouse–No Visitors Allowed." Next-to-last classic old ballyard to put in lights, in 1948. Home plate and batters' boxes oriented towards right-center rather than straight out to the mound. This tends to give righthanded pitchers more outside corner strike calls and can disorient visiting batters. Was known as Bennett Park from 1901 to 1911; wooden structure with field facing opposite way.

BURNS PARK

STYLE: Wooden.
OCCUPANT: AL Tigers, Sunday April 28, 1901 to 1910.
CURRENT USE: Shipping container storage area.
PHENOMENA: Named for George D. Burns, an early president of the Tigers.

COMERICA PARK

CAPACITY: 40,000
STYLE: New Classic.
OCCUPANT: AL Tigers, April 11, 2000 to present.
SURFACE: Grass.
DIMENSIONS: Left Field: 346; Left Center: 402; Center Field: 422; Right Center: 379; Right Field: 330.
PHENOMENA: Park cost "only" $280 million to construct. The scoreboard is the biggest of any major league stadium.

Tigers All-Stars

+ Did not play

1933	Charlie Gehringer		Bobo Newsom
1934	Tommy Bridges+	**1941**	Al Benton+
	Mickey Cochrane		Birdie Tebbetts+
	Charlie Gehringer		Rudy York
1935	Tommy Bridges+	**1942**	Al Benton
	Mickey Cochrane+		Hal Newhouser+
	Charlie Gehringer		Birdie Tebbetts
	Schoolboy Rowe+		Rudy York
1936	Tommy Bridges+	**1943**	Hal Newhouser
	Charlie Gehringer		Dick Wakefield
	Goose Goslin		Rudy York
	Schoolboy Rowe	**1944**	Pinky Higgins
1937	Tommy Bridges		Hal Newhouser
	Charlie Gehringer		Dizzy Trout+
	Hank Greenberg+		Rudy York+
	Gee Walker+	**1945**	Hank Greenberg+
1938	Charlie Gehringer		Eddie Mayo+
	Hank Greenberg+		Hal Newhouser+
	Vern Kennedy+	**1946**	Hal Newhouser
	Rudy York	**1947**	George Kell
1939	Tommy Bridges		Pat Mullin+
	Hank Greenberg		Hal Newhouser
	Bobo Newsom+		Dizzy Trout+
1940	Tommy Bridges+	**1948**	Hoot Evers
	Hank Greenberg		

	George Kell+	**1958**	Al Kaline
	Pat Mullin		Harvey Kuenn+
	Hal Newhouser	**1959**	Jim Bunning
1949	George Kell	**Game 1**	Al Kaline
	Virgil Trucks		Harvey Kuenn
	Vic Wertz	**1959**	Al Kaline
1950	Hoot Evers	**Game 2**	Harvey Kuenn+
	Ted Gray	**1960**	Al Kaline
	Art Houtteman	**Game 1**	Frank Lary
	George Kell	**1960**	Al Kaline
1951	Fred Hutchinson	**Game 2**	Frank Lary
	George Kell	**1961**	Jim Bunning
	Vic Wertz	**Game 1**	Norm Cash
1952	Vic Wertz+		Rocky Colavito
1953	Harvey Kuenn		Al Kaline
1954	Ray Boone		Frank Lary
	Harvey Kuenn+	**1961**	Jim Bunning
1955	Billy Hoeft+	**Game 2**	Norm Cash
	Al Kaline		Rocky Colavito
	Harvey Kuenn		Al Kaline
1956	Ray Boone	**1962**	Hank Aguirre+
	Al Kaline	**Game 1**	Jim Bunning
	Harvey Kuenn		Rocky Colavito
	Charlie Maxwell+	**1962**	Hank Aguirre
1957	Jim Bunning	**Game 2**	Jim Bunning+
	Al Kaline		Rocky Colavito
	Harvey Kuenn		Al Kaline
	Charlie Maxwell	**1963**	Jim Bunning

	Al Kaline		Mickey Lolich
1964	Bill Freehan+	**1972**	Norm Cash
	Al Kaline+		Joe Coleman+
	Jerry Lumpe+		Bill Freehan
1965	Bill Freehan		Mickey Lolich
	Willie Horton	**1973**	Ed Brinkman
	Al Kaline		Bill Freehan+
	Dick McAuliffe		Willie Horton
1966	Norm Cash	**1974**	John Hiller+
	Bill Freehan		Al Kaline
	Al Kaline	**1975**	Bill Freehan+
	Dick McAuliffe	**1976**	Mark Fidrych
	Denny McLain		Ron Le Flore
1967	Bill Freehan		Rusty Staub
	Al Kaline+	**1977**	Mark Fidrych+
	Dick McAuliffe		Jason Thompson+
1968	Bill Freehan	**1978**	Jason Thompson
	Willie Horton	**1979**	Steve Kemp
	Denny McLain	**1980**	Lance Parrish
	Don Wert		Alan Trammell
1969	Bill Freehan	**1981**	Jack Morris
	Mickey Lolich+	**1982**	Lance Parrish
	Denny McLain	**1983**	Aurelio Lopez+
1970	Bill Freehan		Lance Parrish
	Willie Horton		Lou Whitaker
1971	Norm Cash	**1984**	Willie Hernandez
	Bill Freehan		Chet Lemon
	Al Kaline		Jack Morris

	Lance Parrish	**1996**	Travis Fryman
	Alan Trammell+	**1997**	Justin Thompson
	Lou Whitaker	**1998**	Damion Easley
1985	Willie Hernandez	**1999**	Brad Ausmus
	Jack Morris		
	Lance Parrish+		
	Dan Petry		
	Alan Trammell		
	Lou Whitaker		
1986	Willie Hernandez+		
	Lance Parrish		
	Lou Whitaker		
1987	Jack Morris		
	Matt Nokes		
	Alan Trammell		
	Lou Whitaker+		
1988	Doyle Alexander+		
	Alan Trammell+		
1989	Mike Henneman+		
1990	Cecil Fielder		
	Alan Trammell		
1991	Cecil Fielder		
1992	Travis Fryman		
1993	Cecil Fielder		
	Travis Fryman		
1994	Travis Fryman		
	Mickey Tettleton		
1995	David Wells		

Biographies of Tigers Greats

SPARKY ANDERSON Manager
Cin N 1970-78, Det A 1979-95

Sparky Anderson was the first manager to win a World Series in each league and only the seventh skipper to reach 2,000 career wins. He piloted both the Detroit Tigers and the Cincinnati Reds to more victories than any previous manager, and he was the first manager to have 100-win seasons with two different teams. Sparky was a Manager of the Year selection twice in each league.

Anderson often claimed that managers play a limited role. "There's never been a good manager in the history of the game," he said, "but there have been some great players." Anderson's ebullient optimism and sometimes outrageous hyperbole often overshadowed his managing, bringing to mind Casey Stengel, to whom Anderson was often compared for his winning ways and nonstop mouth. The pipe-puffing Anderson often made contradictory statements; all the same, most observers agreed that he believed what he said.

In 1959, Anderson batted .218 with 12 extra-base hits as the Phillies' regular second baseman in his only season in the majors as a player. As a manager, Anderson led what became known as the Big Red Machine to two world championships before he was fired in 1978.

He took over a renascent Detroit team from Les Moss on June 14, 1979. Under Anderson, youngsters Alan Trammell, Lou

Whitaker, Kirk Gibson, Lance Parrish, Jack Morris, and Dan Petry blossomed. The Tigers posted winning records during Sparky's first four seasons, then exploded in 1984. That year the Tigers started out 35-5 on the way to a club-record 104 wins, a sweep of the Royals in the ALCS, and a five-game World Series victory over San Diego.

After a pair of third-place finishes, the Tigers overtook Toronto in the last week of the 1987 season, sweeping the Blue Jays in Detroit on the final weekend for the Eastern Division title. Detroit was upset in the ALCS by the Twins, but Anderson's 34-21 postseason record and .619 winning percentage stands as second-best in history. In 1989 Anderson took several weeks off during the season because of nervous exhaustion. He returned to manage the Tigers through 1995 with limited success.

TOMMY BRIDGES Pitcher
Det A 1930-43, 1945-46

Tommy Bridges, son of a Tennessee country doctor, was expected to follow in his father's profession. Instead, despite his lack of size at 5 feet 10 inches and 155 pounds, he became one of the best pitchers in baseball.

Bridges became a regular for the Tigers in 1931. On August 5, 1932, he came within one out of pitching a perfect game against Washington. In 1934 Bridges started a string of three straight 20-victory years, going 22-11 in 1934, 21-10 in 1935, and 23-11 in 1936. He was selected for the All-Star Game all three years. "One of the best curveball pitchers I ever saw. I always said I was glad I didn't have to hit against him," teammate Charlie Gehringer said in his praises.

Sometimes, however, Bridges was alleged to have less than sanitary pitches in his repertoire. Bridges remained a key starter for the Tigers through the 1943 season when, at age 37, he was called into the military.

JIM BUNNING Pitcher
Det A 1955-63, Phi N 1964-67, 1970-71, Pit N 1968-69, LA N 1969

The highlight of Jim Bunning's career came—appropriately for a parent of seven—on Father's Day. On June 21, 1964, Bunning, of the Philadelphia Phillies, pitched the first regular-season perfect game since Charlie Robertson of the Chicago White Sox had done it on April 30, 1922. Using a state-of-the-art slider and a sweeping sidearm delivery that contorted his body so that his glove hand dusted the mound, Bunning shut down the New York Mets, 6-0, at Shea Stadium with the first perfect game tossed in the National League since 1880.

With a reputation for a live fastball, Bunning first signed with the Detroit Tigers and made the majors midway through the 1955 season. Bunning quickly realized that a good fastball was not enough to get big league hitters out. "I think I had to make an adjustment early," he said. "In 1956, I started getting a good breaking ball. That was the winter I went to the Cuban Winter League and pitched for the Marianao club and worked on a slider."

His extra work paid off. In nine years with Detroit, Bunning won 118 games, and in 1957, his first season in the rotation, he led the AL in wins, posting a 20-8 mark with a 2.69 ERA. That year he was selected to the first of his seven All-Star Games. On July 20, 1958, Bunning recorded his first no-hitter, against the Boston Red Sox.

After 1963, Bunning was traded to Philadelphia and went on to win more than 100 games in the National league with Philadelphia, Pittsburgh, Los Angeles, and Philadelphia again. After retiring, Bunning launched a career in politics by serving in the Kentucky state legislature; later he was elected to Congress, but then lost a bid to become governor of Kentucky. In 1996 he won election to the Hall of Fame and two years later to the United States Senate.

DONIE BUSH Shortstop
Det A 1908-21, Was A 1921-23

Donie Bush spent 65 years in organized baseball as a player, manager, scout, and owner. He had just a sixth-grade education, but he was brilliant by baseball standards.

He used his keen knowledge of the strike zone to lead the American League in walks in five of his first six full professional seasons. With Hall of Famers Ty Cobb and Sam Crawford-and later Harry Heilmann-batting behind him, Bush scored 90 or more runs in eight of his first nine full seasons. Bush led the American League with 112 runs in 1917. He was a skillful basestealer as well and finished his career with 404 stolen bases.

NORM CASH First Base
Chi A 1958-59, Det A 1960-74

In 1961 Tigers first baseman Norm Cash had a season to

remember. Cash hit .361 in 1961 to lead the league by 37 points, with an on-base percentage of .488 and a slugging average of .662. Along with his 41 homers, his 193 hits led the league, and he drove in 132 runs, scored 119, and walked 124 times.

Much later in his career, Cash attributed his success to a corked bat and went so far as to doctor a bat for *Sports Illustrated*. As a result, his 36-ounce bat felt like a 34-ounce model, providing extra power.

After his stellar 1961 season, Cash's batting average fell to .243 in 1962, the largest drop in history by a batting champion. Cash never again hit above .283 in 13 more seasons in the big leagues. It was his consistent power, solid fielding, and fun-loving personality that kept him in the majors. Cash belted 25 homers for the Tigers in their 1968 championship year and was their leading batsman in the World Series, hitting .385.

TY COBB Outfield/Manager
Det A 1905-26, Phi A 1927-28

In 1936 Cobb was the first man elected to Cooperstown, mostly by voters who grew up in his era. Babe Ruth was second. The majority of today's critics would reverse the order and maybe drop Cobb a few more pegs besides. The reason, of course, is that the modern game, with its emphasis on home runs, has evolved in a Ruthian rather than a Cobbian direction.

Cobb's strengths were his ability to reach first, steal a base or two, and then score. After all these years, he's still first in batting average (.366), second in hits (4,189), fourth in steals (892), and first in runs (2,245). He collected ten AL batting titles, hit over .400 three times, led in steals six times and in runs five. In other words, he was the best at the things he tried to be best at.

He was no home run hitter, managing only 118 in 24 seasons. But for most of those seasons, going for homers against the dead ball was a losing proposition. He did lead in slugging average eight times, proving he wasn't just a powder-puff hitter. Admittedly, for all his heavy hitting, Ty's Tigers won only three pennants and no World Series. In 19 of his 22 seasons in Detroit, the Tabbies missed the brass ring. The fault, dear Brutus, was not in their star; it was on their pitcher's mound. Cobb was the best player of his time-or at least the first two-thirds of his time.

Now, if the critics want to stomp on Cobb, they can put their clod-hoppers on his personality. "The Georgia Peach" was no peach. He was mean, vindictive, selfish, vain, a bully, a racist, paranoid, cruel, and hot-tempered. He spiked infielders just for the hell of it, fought—that is, physically attacked-anyone who crossed him, would do literally anything to be first in literally anything.

"We may never see his like again," Connie Mack once said of him. Indeed we won't.

MICKEY COCHRANE Catcher/Manager
Phi A 1925-33, Det A 1934-37

They used to argue who was the greatest catcher ever, Cochrane or Bill Dickey. Modern statistical techniques have moved Gabby Hartnett into the discussion. Josh Gibson has his backers. And later ages shout the praises of Yogi Berra and Johnny Bench. But the final cut usually comes down to "Mickey Cochrane or..."

When Mickey gets the edge, it's usually on "leadership," which is measured as easily as the distance to Oz. Nevertheless, Cochrane played on five AL pennant winners in a seven-year stretch, and that's at least tertiary evidence that he was officer material. As a matter of fact, he managed two of those teams (Detroit in 1934-1935) while taking his regular turn behind the plate.

From the time he made his debut with the Athletics, through his sale to the Tigers for $100,000 in 1934, until a Bump Hadley pitch ended his career and nearly killed him in 1937, Black Mike averaged .320, the best career mark for any catcher. He had good speed for a catcher (64 stolen bases) and usually batted second. He scored 1,041 runs—four times over 100. He was a line drive hitter, but in 1932, when he drove in 112 runs, he also knocked 23 homers. He won Most Valuable Player Awards in 1928 and 1934, although neither year was his best with a bat. He was named to the Hall of Fame in 1947.

SAM CRAWFORD   Outfield
Cin N 1899-1902, Det A 1903-17

Outfielder Sam Crawford was one of the greatest all-around players of the Dead Ball Era. Although overshadowed in the public eye by teammate Ty Cobb, "Wahoo Sam" was nearly Cobb's equal on offense and vastly superior on defense. Crawford's 309 career triples are a record that will stand forever unless baseball undergoes a revolutionary change.

Sam hit .333 with a league-leading 22 triples in 1902, establishing himself as one of the NL's best young hitters. A contract offer of $3,500, considerably more than the Reds were paying, convinced Crawford to become a Detroit Tiger. He proved a bargain in 1903 as he hit .335, knocked in 89 RBIs, and smacked 25 triples.

Ty Cobb arrived in Detroit in 1905 and Cobb and Crawford soon became the league's most potent one-two batting punch. In 1907 they led the Tigers to their first pennant. Crawford hit .323 and led the league in runs scored, but Detroit lost the World Series to the Chicago Cubs of Tinker-Evers-Chance fame in five games.

The Tigers repeated as league champions in 1908, but again fell to the Cubs in the Fall Classic. Crawford led the league that year with seven home runs and finished second to Cobb with 184 hits, 270 total bases, 80 RBIs, a .311 batting average, and a .457 slugging average. Detroit won its third straight pennant in 1909 as Crawford led the league with 35 doubles and finished second to Cobb with 266 total bases, 97 RBIs, and a slugging average of .452. From 1910 through 1915 Crawford led the league in triples four times. He led in RBIs three times, topping 100 in five of the six years.

Crawford compiled a career batting average of .309 and 1,525 RBIs. Cobb campaigned to have him enshrined in the Hall of Fame, and succeeded in 1957.

HOOKS DAUSS Pitcher
Det A 1912-26

Ask someone to name the all-time Detroit Tigers' leader in victories, and they're likely to guess Jim Bunning, Mickey Lolich, Hal

Newhouser, Denny McLain, or Jack Morris. The correct answer is George "Hooks" Dauss, a right-hander who pitched for the club from 1912 through 1926.

When Dauss retired he owned 222 victories, illustrating the skill and heart of a man who was once released by a minor league club before getting a chance to show what he could do. Anyone who dismissed Dauss because of his size or for any other reason had 15 years in which to watch and regret. In a career spent entirely with the Tigers, Dauss won in double figures for 14 consecutive seasons, even though the Tigers finished higher than third only twice. Three times he reached the 20-victory plateau, and on another occasion he won 19. His 538 appearances rank second all-time among Tigers.

BILL DONOVAN   Pitcher
Was N 1898, Bro N 1899-1902, Det A 1903-12, 1918, NY A 1915-16

While on his way to attend baseball's annual winter meetings in 1923, "Wild Bill" Donovan died in a train wreck in Forsyth, N.Y. So ended a life spent in baseball, a life in which he pitched 18 major league seasons, compiled a 186-139 mark, and appeared in three World Series. Twice Donovan won 25 games, and from 1901 through 1908 he won at least 17 games in seven out of eight seasons. He also featured two managerial stints on his resume.

In 1907 Donovan matched his career high with 25 victories against just four losses, for a league-leading winning percentage of .862. Only three other AL pitchers have posted a better winning percentage. Ed Killian's 25 wins and George Mullin's 20 gave the

Tigers three 20-game winners in 1907, and Detroit won the pennant by four games. In 1910 and 1911 Donovan had winning seasons, but his arm gave way in 1912.

DARRELL EVANS   Third Base/First Base
Atl N 1969-76, 1989, SF N 1976-83, Det A 1984-88

Like fine wine, third baseman Darrell Evans seemed to get better with age. He became, at 38, the oldest player to win a home run title and the second-oldest to hit 40 homers in a season as he put a cap on a fine career that saw him collect 414 homers. Evans hit for power but not for average and was a career .248 hitter, so he could easily be stereotyped as a free-swinging slugger. Actually, he was quite selective at the plate, and during the course of his career walked more times than he struck out, 1,605 versus 1,410.

With Detroit, he shifted between first base and designated hitter. In 1984 he had an off year but, in 1985, he rebounded, hitting a league-leading 40 homers. At age 40 in 1987 he hit 34 homers, topping Hank Sauer's previous record of 26 at that age. He hit 22 homers in 1988 but found no major league club willing to sign him for the following season.

CECIL FIELDER   First Base/DH
Tor A 1985-88, Det A 1990-96, NY A 1996-97, Ana A 1998,
Cle A 1998

Cecil Fielder began the decade of the 1990s as the personification of home run heroism. "Big Daddy" averaged 36 home runs and 113 RBIs from 1990 to 1996, mostly in a Detroit Tigers uniform.

Fielder broke into the majors in 1985 but failed to establish himself. In 1989 he left the majors to play for Japan's Hanshin Tigers, where he hit 38 home runs in just 106 games. Although few players had ever returned from Japan and excelled in the major leagues, Detroit signed the slugger. He drove in 132 runs, the first of three straight RBI titles. His 51 homers were the most in the AL since 1961.

Fielder led the AL again with 44 homers and 133 RBIs in 1991. He was runner-up in the balloting for MVP for the second consecutive year, and the Tigers rewarded him with the richest contract in baseball history to that point. As Detroit sunk below the .500 mark, Fielder publicly called for a change of scenery. In July 1996 Detroit dealt him to the New York Yankees, then in a tight battle for first place in the AL East. Fielder hit 13 homers down the stretch for New York. He batted .308 in the postseason—including a .391 mark in the World Series—as the Yankees claimed their first championship since 1978.

BILL FREEHAN Catcher
Det A 1961, 1963-76

Bill Freehan is the catcher many other American League receivers measured themselves against during the late 1960s. An 11-time All-Star, he has the highest lifetime fielding percentage of any catcher in history, .993, tied with Elston Howard. Freehan was responsible for handling what developed into an outstanding Detroit pitching staff that included Denny McLain and Mickey Lolich.

The 6-foot-2 righthanded hitter was the consummate team player. He played through leg injuries and back trouble and in 1968 set a new league record by getting hit with pitches 24 times. That year the Tigers won the pennant by 12 games as Denny McLain won 31 games and Freehan contributed 25 home runs.

In the World Series, Detroit had fallen behind St. Louis three games to one. In Game 5 Freehan, despite hitting only .083 for the Series, made a key play at the plate during the fifth inning when Lou Brock tried to score from second on Julian Javier's single to left. Willie Horton threw in to Freehan. Brock came in standing up to try to jar the ball loose, but umpire Doug Harvey signaled him out. Many believe that Freehan's play turned the Series around; the Tigers won in seven dramatic games. Freehan later served as base-ball coach at the University of Michigan.

TRAVIS FRYMAN   Third Base
Det A 1990-97, Cle A 1998-99

Travis Fryman began his professional career in the Detroit organization as a shortstop with no power, but he blossomed into a power-hitting third baseman in the major leagues. He played both short and third for his first three years for the Tigers, who signed him to a lucrative five-year contract after 1993.

While he made the All-Star team four times in five years, he never matured into the franchise-caliber player the team expected. Detroit traded Fryman during the 1997 expansion draft to Arizona for three players. Two weeks later, Arizona dealt Fryman to Cleveland. Fryman hit a career-high 28 homers in his first season with the Indians, but suffered through an injury-shortened 1999.

CHARLIE GEHRINGER Second Base
Det A 1924-42

They called second baseman Charlie Gehringer "the Mechanical Man" because of the quiet, methodical way he went about his business. Outfielder Doc Cramer remarked, "You wind him up on Opening Day and forget about him."

Gehringer played in the All-Star Game the first six times the Midseason Classic occurred, hit .320 lifetime, collected more than 200 hits in a season seven times, and led the AL in fielding seven times. During one 14-season span the consistent Gehringer fell under .300 only once, in 1932, when he plummeted all the way to .298. According to Gehringer, "That was the year I was going to be Babe Ruth. I think I had eight (home runs) before he had any, and I began going for the fences. I wound up getting not many homers—and not many hits either."

Gehringer's best year was 1937 when he led the AL with a .371 average and won the MVP. Gehringer was named to the Hall of Fame in 1949.

"I wasn't a rabble rouser," he said. "I wasn't a big noisemaker in the infield, which a lot of managers think you've got to be or you're not showing an interest. But I don't think it contributes much. You can't talk your way into a batting championship."

On Aug. 10, 1951, the Tigers appointed him as their general manager and vice president. He held the general manager's post until October 1953 but retained the Detroit vice presidency through 1959.

KIRK GIBSON Outfield
Det A 1979-87, 1993-95, LA N 1988-90, KC A 1991, Pit N 1992

The Michigan native was an All-America wide receiver at Michigan State, but he signed to play baseball with his hometown Detroit Tigers. By the early 1980s Gibbie was reviving the dormant franchise with his ferocious enthusiasm, sprinter speed, and roof-top power. In 1984 Gibson slugged 27 homers with 91 RBIs as Detroit won 104 games. Gibson smashed two homers in the decisive Game 5 of the World Series against San Diego. His memorable three-run clout in the eighth helped insure Detroit's first world championship since 1968.

Over the next three seasons with Detroit, Gibson belted 29, 28, and 24 homers—and stole 30, 34, and 26 bases. He moved to Los Angeles as a free agent, and was named MVP in his first season in the NL despite his relatively low total of 76 RBIs. He proved his value to the team by leading the undermanned Dodgers past the heavily favored New York Mets in the NLCS and then turning the World Series upside-down with one stupendously unlikely home run.

Injuries plagued Gibson in his final two more years in Los Angeles. He revived his career with the Tigers with 23 home runs in just 98 games in strike-shortened 1994. He retired after the 1995 season, but later joined the club's broadcast team. Gibson never played in an All-Star Game.

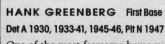

HANK GREENBERG First Base
Det A 1930, 1933-41, 1945-46, Pit N 1947

One of the most fearsome home run hitters of all time, Greenberg played only nine full seasons, yet amassed 331 homers and 1,276 RBIs. Although he was an impressive six-four and 210 pounds, his success stemmed more from hard work than natural gifts. Thought too tall and awkward to play baseball, he applied himself with diligence and made himself into an adequate defensive first baseman. In 1940, when the Tigers wanted to get Rudy York's bat into the lineup, Hank went to left field, and did the job well enough that the Tigers won the pennant.

In 1934 he led the Tigers to the World Series with 26 homers, 139 RBIs, and a league-leading 63 doubles. In 1935 he was even better, winning his first MVP Award with 36 home runs and 170 RBIs, both leading the AL. The Tigers were world champions. In 1937 he came back with 40 home runs and 183 RBIs, the third-highest RBI total ever. Perhaps his 1938 season is his most famous. That year he chased Babe Ruth's record down to the wire, finishing with 58 home runs. Two years later, he won his second MVP on 41 homers and 150 RBIs, and the Tigers again won the pennant.

Then in 1941, only 19 games into the season, Greenberg was inducted into the Army. He was 31. He did not return to the Tigers until midway through 1945. Fittingly his ninth-inning grand slam on the final day of the season won Detroit another pennant. After once more leading the AL in homers (with 44) and RBIs (with 127) in 1946, he was sold to Pittsburgh before the 1947 season for $75,000. The Pirates shortened the distant left field fence at Forbes Field in his honor by erecting a bullpen, quickly labeled "Greenberg Gardens." Hank hit 25 homers in 1947, then retired. Greenberg was elected to the Hall of Fame in 1956.

HARRY HEILMANN Outfield
Det A 1914, 1916-29, Cin N 1930, 1932

Heilmann was a good hitter who became a great hitter when the lively ball was introduced in 1920. Line drives that fielders had previously reached began whizzing by their gloves before they could react, and Harry was a line-drive machine. His homer totals were only average (his biggest year was 21 in 1923) but he hit plenty of gappers for doubles and triples. For much of his career the righthanded hitter batted behind Ty Cobb, helping him to his all-time record in runs scored. Harry had 1,538 RBIs and topped 100 in eight seasons.

"Slug" didn't help his team in the outfield. He was slow and awkward. For two years the Tigers tried to put him at first base. He led AL first basemen in errors both years, so they sent him back to the outfield, where Heilmann had fewer opportunities to be slow and awkward.

But with a bat in his hand, Heilmann rivaled the NL's Rogers Hornsby as the greatest righthanded hitter of the time. He led the AL in hitting four times: in 1921, with .394; in 1923 it was .403; in 1925, .393; and in 1927, .398. In his "off-years" between titles, he bided his time with .356, .346, and .367. His career average was a remarkable .342.

Heilmann was a low-key, articulate man, who told droll stories of his playing days. After retiring, he put those talents to work as a popular play-by-play radio broadcaster for the Tigers. He was named to the Hall of Fame in 1952.

MIKE HENNEMAN Pitcher
Det A 1987-95, Hou N 1995, Tex A 1996

Henneman made his debut during Detroit's division-winning season of 1987, winning 11 games and losing only three in middle relief. With the decline of Willie Hernandez, he soon graduated to closing, crafting a 1.87 ERA and saving 22 games in his sophomore season. Mike followed with an All-Star year in 1989, winning 11 against only four defeats, as the veteran Detroit club disintegrated with 103 losses.

The righthander saved 91 games from 1990 through 1993, including a 10-2 season in 1991. He finished his career with 31 shaky saves in Texas in 1996, as he went 0-7 with a 5.79 ERA. His 154 saves in Detroit are the team's career-best.

WILLIE HERNANDEZ Pitcher
Chi N 1977-83, Phi N 1983, Det A 1984-89

Hernandez, who late in his career eschewed the Anglo form of his given name and insisted on being called "Guillermo," made the transformation from a setup pitcher in 1983 to a relief ace in 1984 when he helped pitch Sparky Anderson's Detroit Tigers to a world championship. Throwing screwballs, sinking fastballs, and quick-breaking curves, Hernandez baffled AL hitters. At one point he converted a then-record 32 consecutive save opportunities.

AL hitters were no match for Hernandez's nasty stuff in 1984. He went 9-3 with a 1.92 ERA, led the league in appearances with 80, and won both the MVP and Cy Young Awards. In 1985-86,

Hernandez recorded back-to-back 30-save seasons. The following season he saved 24 games.

JOHN HILLER Pitcher
Det A 1965-70, 1972-80

John Hiller won the 1973 Comeback Player of the Year Award, but he might be the comeback player of the century. In 1971 the lefthanded pitcher suffered a massive stroke and was subsequently released by the Tigers. Determined to return to the game, in 1972 Hiller took a job as the Tigers' batting-practice pitcher. Management was impressed enough to place him back on the active roster on July 8, 1972. In 1973 he recorded 38 saves, a major league record at the time, and won Fireman of the Year and became famous for his devasting changeup.

A bullpen pitcher who made an occasional start, Hiller was 23-19 with 13 saves in four full seasons before his stroke. He returned at age 29 to save three games and win one with a 2.03 ERA. During the next seven seasons, he went 63-55 with 109 saves for Detroit.

WILLIE HORTON Outfield/DH
Det A 1963-77, Tex A 1977, Cle A 1978, Oak A 1978,
Tor A 1978, Sea A 1979-80

Outfielder Willie Horton was a longtime fan favorite in Detroit, rewarding their affection by four times leading the club in RBIs and three times in homers. But he not only performed on the field. During the 1967 Detroit riots, Horton did his part to help restore order, climbing onto a truck to exhort fellow African-Americans to desist from looting and violence.

Reared in inner-city Detroit, Horton was a highly-scouted high school prospect, particularly after he launched a homer into Tiger Stadium's right field stands as a 16-year-old. He signed with the Tigers in August 1961, and was brought up to Detroit at the end of the 1963 season. He singled as a pinch hitter in his first major league at bat. Then he smacked a pinch homer off Robin Roberts his second time up. In 15 games he hit .326 but spent most of the 1964 season at Syracuse, where he hit 28 homers.

Horton became a regular in the Tigers outfield in 1965, hitting 29 homers and driving in 104 runs. On June 22, 1966, he hit his first major league grand slam, and he finished the season with 27 round-trippers and 100 RBIs. Hampered in 1967 by ankle problems, so serious they required surgery, Horton bounced back in 1968 to slug a career-high 36 homers.

In the 1968 World Series, Horton batted .304. In Game 5, however, it was Horton's fielding that loomed large. In the fifth inning, with the Cardinals ahead, 3-2, and Lou Brock on second, Julian Javier singled to left. Horton's throw to catcher Bill Freehan was waiting for Brock, who inexplicably chose not to slide. Coming in standing up, he was an easy out. The play kept the Tigers in the game, which they eventually won, 5-3.

Used exclusively at DH by the Mariners in 1979, Horton hit 29 homers and drove in 106 runs and earned *The Sporting News* AL Comeback Player of the Year award.

HUGHIE JENNINGS Manager
Det A 1907-20, NY N 1924-25

A law school graduate, Jennings played on the famous rip 'n' run Baltimore Orioles of the Gay Nineties as their shortstop and captain. Hughie took over as Detroit manager in 1907 and won pennants in his first three seasons. Only Ralph Houk of the Yankees matched that. In 11 more years of trying, Jennings never won again, but he finished in the first division seven times. His greatest player was, of course, Ty Cobb, whom he disliked but coddled. His other players were treated sternly, often sarcastically. Cobb eventually replaced him as manager.

Jennings' nickname was "Eeyah," because he used to shout it from the coaching box. The most commonly reprinted photo of Jennings shows the freckle-faced redhead in mid-stamp-eyes ablaze, mouth twisted in a snarl. If photos could talk, that one would be screaming his trademark, baffling "Ee-yah!" Among other possible explanations, Hughie said it was Hawaiian for "Watch out!"

In 1945 the Veterans Committee named him to the Hall of Fame. His plaque cites both his play as a shortstop and the pennants he won as a manager.

AL KALINE Outfield
Det A 1953-74

Albert William Kaline Kaline never spent a minute in the minor leagues. A Baltimore native, he was signed by the Detroit

Tigers out of high school for $30,000 in 1953 and went straight to the majors. The following season, at age 19, Kaline joined the starting lineup and hit .276. He was blessed with all the tools a good ballplayer needed, and Detroit fans felt it was merely a matter of time before he became one of the game's great stars.

It didn't take Kaline long. In 1955, at age 20, he became the youngest player to win a batting title when he hit .340, belted 27 home runs, and knocked in 102 runs. In the outfield, his defense was superb. Kaline looked as if he were Detroit's equivalent of Willie Mays or Mickey Mantle, and for a few years he was. From 1955 to 1963 he hit at least .300 in all but two seasons. But Kaline was continually dogged by injuries that kept him out of the lineup for 10 or 15 games a season. He never quite had the power of his counterparts or their physical ability. Said Kaline once of Mantle, "I wish I was half the ballplayer he is."

He never won another batting title and he never led the league in home runs or RBIs. In another city Kaline's performance might have disappointed the fans, but the loyal Detroit followers didn't complain. They appreciated Kaline's work ethic and modesty. Like many in the city, Kaline did his job, did it well, and did it without grumbling. That was enough in Detroit. The Yankees won the pennant almost every season anyway, so Kaline gave Detroit someone to cheer for.

In 1962 Kaline appeared to be on his way to a career year, but on May 26 in Yankee Stadium he did a somersault to make a game-ending catch and broke his collarbone. Despite missing nearly two months of play, Kaline finished with a career-high 29 home runs, with 94 RBIs in only 398 at bats.

He tied his career high with 29 homers in 1966, and was on pace to break that mark in 1967. But with Detroit finally challenging for the pennant, Kaline broke his hand and missed a month of the season. He finished with 28 homers as the Tigers lost the pennant to Boston on the final day of the season.

However, in 1968 the Tigers got off to a fast start and coasted to the pennant, defeating Baltimore by 12 games. Kaline was hit in May by a pitch that broke his arm, and he was out of the lineup for a month. When he returned, he didn't hit well and saw only part-time duty the rest of the season. To get Kaline into the lineup for the World Series, manager Mayo Smith took a daring and brilliant gamble: playing center fielder Mickey Stanley at short stop and moving right fielder Jim Northrup to center.

The strategy paid off and helped Detroit win the Series. Although pitcher Denny McLain stumbled against Cardinals ace Bob Gibson, Mickey Lolich was magnificent and won three games. Kaline hit .379 for the Series, smacked two home runs, led both teams with eight RBIs, and made several sparkling plays in the field. Both Northrup and Stanley were also superb defensively, and Detroit won in seven games.

A late-career move to designated hitter allowed Kaline to play long enough to reach 3,000 hits. Al retired at the end of the season with 3,007 hits, 399 home runs, and a .297 batting average in 22 major league seasons, all with Detroit. He ranks third in major league history for the longest career spent with one team. Kaline was a member of 15 All-Star teams and won 11 Gold Gloves.

Mr. Tiger was elected to the Hall of Fame in 1980 in his first eligible year. On Aug. 17, 1980, the Tigers retired his uniform No. 6.

GEORGE KELL   Third Base
Phi A 1943-46, Det A 1946-52, Bos A 1952-54, Chi A 1954-56, Bal A 1956-57

Kell gave the Tigers and several other AL clubs some steady fielding and .300 hitting after World War II. He led the league in batting average in 1949, just inching out Ted Williams by .0002 with a .3429 mark. Kell was safely in front of Williams as he approached his last at-bat of the season. Teammates urged him to let a pinch hitter bat in his place since an out would lose him the title. He refused and took his place in the on-deck circle, but before he could bat a teammate ended the inning and the season by hitting into a double play.

In nine seasons, Kell batted over .300. Never a power hitter, Kell is one of the few modern hitters to have over 100 RBIs with fewer than 10 home runs, a feat he achieved in 1950. In the field, George had an excellent throwing arm and was sure-handed. He led AL third basemen in fielding average seven times, in assists four times, and in putouts and double plays twice.

In 1983, Kell was named to the Hall of Fame. He also spent 31 years in the television booth calling the play-by-play on Tigers telecasts, most of them as a partner with fellow Hall of Famer Al Kaline.

HARVEY KUENN Outfield/Shortstop
Det A 1952-59, Cle A 1960, SF N 1961-65, Chi N 1965-66, Phi N 1966

An aggressive player capable of making the spectacular play and muffing the easy one, Harvey Kuenn, a lifetime .303 hitter, won AL Rookie of the Year honors in 1953 and played on six All-Star teams. The Tigers right-hander led the league in hits four times and doubles three times, and in 1959 he topped the list in batting average when he hit .353. He returned to his native Milwaukee as a coach and manager and in 1982 led the Brewers to the World Series.

In April 1960, the Tigers traded batting champ Kuenn to Cleveland for slugger Rocky Colavito; Kuenn later was converted to the outfield. He has the dubious distinction of making the last out in two of Sandy Koufax's no-hitters.

FRANK LARY Pitcher
Det A 1954-64, NY N 1964-65, Mil N 1964, Chi A 1965

Detroit righthander Frank "Taters" Lary earned the reputation as the 1950s premier "Yankee Killer," going 5-1 against the Bronx Bombers in 1956 and 7-0 in 1958. Lifetime, Lary was 27-13 against New York.

Frank Strong Lary led the AL in wins in 1956 and won a Gold Glove in 1961. He also led the league in innings pitched and complete games three times. In three All-Star Games he allowed no earned runs. Frank developed a sore arm in 1962 and was ineffective for the rest of his career. He finished with a 128-116 record and a 3.49 ERA.

RON LeFLORE Outfield
Det A 1974-79, Mon N 1980, Chi A 1981-82

Few major leaguers traveled as hard a road as Ron LeFlore. When the Tigers first scouted him, LeFlore was in a maximum-security prison for armed robbery. A year later, he was Detroit's starting center fielder. Perhaps the fastest man in baseball in the mid-1970s, LeFlore led both leagues in stolen bases and hit .300 three times. Incredibly, he had never played baseball—only softball—until May 18, 1971. He quickly made up for lost time.

LeFlore got a chance because a fellow prisoner was a friend of a Detroit bar owner who knew Detroit manager Billy Martin. Martin agreed to give LeFlore a tryout on a 48-hour furlough in June 1973 at Tiger Stadium, where Ron hit balls into the upper deck and impressed with his speed and his arm.

In 1976, LeFlore hit .316, swiped 58 bases, scored 93 runs, and put together a 30-game hitting streak, the longest in the AL since Joe DiMaggio's 34-game streak in 1949. In 1978, he led the AL in stolen bases with 68 and in runs with 126. The 31-year-old LeFlore stole 78 bases and batted .300 in 1979, but on Dec. 7 he was traded to Montreal for pitcher Dan Schatzeder. The following season LeFlore stole 97 bases and had an outside chance of breaking Lou Brock's record until his arm was broken by a pitch in early September. He spent his final two seasons with the Chicago White Sox.

LeFlore's life story was published as *Breakout-From Prison to the Big Leagues*, and was later made into a television movie called *One in a Million*.

CHET LEMON   Outfield
Chi A 1975-81, Det A 1982-90

Although Lemon was a third baseman in the minors, the White Sox shifted him to center field where he became a Chicago regular from 1976 through 1981. In 1977 Lemon set AL records for most putouts and chance by an outfielder. He played the field with aplomb, becoming a fan favorite as he patrolled the vast stretches of Comiskey Park.

After 1981, Lemon was traded to Detroit for outfielder Steve Kemp. His best year in Detroit was the Tigers' dream season of 1984: accommodating Kirk Gibson on defense by moving to right field, Lemon enjoyed another All-Star season in which he hit .287 with 20 home runs. Although he went 0-for-13 in the ALCS, he scored the only run in Game 3 as Detroit swept K.C. In the Tigers' five-game victory over San Diego in the World Series, Lemon went 5-for-17 (.294) and fielded flawlessly.

After 1987, injuries and lack of production cut down his playing time. He finished with a career average of .273, 1,875 hits, 215 home runs, and 884 RBIs.

MICKEY LOLICH   Pitcher
Det A 1963-75, NY N 1976, SD N 1978-79

Michael Stephen Lolich was born righthanded but, when a motorcycle fell on him as a toddler and broke his left shoulder, a doctor recommended he throw lefthanded to straighten it out.

In 1963 the Tigers promoted the 22-year-old Lolich. He pitched well for eight years and seemed to reach a new level in 1971 when he led the league with 25 wins, 308 strikeouts, and 29 complete games. In 1972, he had 22 wins. Along the way, the portly southpaw used the 1968 World Series to upstage moundsmen Denny McLain and Bob Gibson in their greatest seasons by winning three games.

Lolich had gone 17-9 with 197 strikeouts in '68 as teammate McLain had earned the Cy Young Award, going 31-6 with 280 strikeouts and a 1.96 ERA. Gibson, the NL Cy Young winner, had gone 22-9 with 268 strikeouts and a minuscule 1.12 ERA. Mickey pitched complete-game wins in Games 2 and 5. Tigers manager Mayo Smith, down three games to two, brought McLain back to pitch Game 6 and gave Lolich the Game 7 assignment against Gibson. Pitching on two days' rest, Lolich outdueled Gibson 4-1 in St. Louis to clinch the championship.

After 1975, the Tigers traded Lolich to the Mets for Rusty Staub. Lolich pitched for 16 years, won 217 games, and struck out 2,832.

AURELIO LOPEZ Pitcher
KC A 1974, StL N 1978, Det A 1979-85, Hou N 1986-87

Known affectionately as "Senor Smoke" for his big fastball, Lopez was Detroit's closer in 1979 and 1980 as well as in 1983, when he was an All-Star. Although little-remembered now, he also held that role at the start of 1984, with Willie Hernandez being relegated to setup duty for the first month. In May, though, Sparky Anderson reversed the two pitchers' roles as Hernandez went on to win the MVP and the Cy Young.

Aurelio started his pro career in his native Mexico. After a brief trial with K.C. in 1970, he led the Mexican League in appearances from 1975 through 1977. Selected the 1977 Mexican League MVP, he was sold to the Cardinals in October of that year. St. Louis traded him in December 1978 to Detroit.

In the 1984 World Series, Lopez won the final game against San Diego. He finished his career with 93 saves and a 62-36 record.

HEINIE MANUSH   Outfield
Det A 1923-27, StL A 1928-30, Was A 1930-35, Bos A 1936, Bro N 1937-38, Pit N 1938-39

A lefthanded batter and thrower, Manush platooned in the Tigers outfield with the aging Bobby Veach in 1923, his first major league season. Detroit manager Ty Cobb, the greatest hitter of the "slash-and-poke era," counseled Manush against swinging for the longball. "Choke up on the bat, hit line drives," Cobb told Manush. Heinie listened and learned so well that, during his 17 major league seasons, he batted .330. Six times he rapped more than 40 doubles, leading the league twice. In eight years he hit more than 10 triples, including years of 20, 18, and 17.

After the 1926 season, George Moriarty replaced Cobb (soon implicated in a gambling scandal) as manager. Manush, a Cobb devotee, didn't get along with Moriarty, and his average slumped to .298. Manush wanted out, and he got his wish in December 1927 when he was dealt to the St. Louis Browns. Manush found Sportsman's Park to his liking and repeated his .378 average of two years earlier. However, Washington's Goose Goslin, with nearly 150 fewer plate appearances than Manush, took the batting title in his final at bat of the year.

Manush finished third in the 1929 batting race with a .355 mark; his .336 average in 1933 was only three points behind league-leader Jimmie Foxx. Heinie also finished third in the AL batting race in 1934 behind Lou Gehrig and Charlie Gehringer. In 1964, he was voted into the Hall of Fame.

DICK McAULIFFE Second Base/Shortstop
Det A 1960-73, Bos A 1974-75

McAuliffe consistently posted high on-base averages with decent power despite his unorthodox batting stance. The left-handed-hitting infielder held his bat parallel to the ground, waist-high, with his front foot dangling in the air.

Richard John McAuliffe arrived in Detroit in 1960. In 1963 he became the Tigers' regular shortstop. He hit a career-high 24 homers in 1964 and was selected to the AL All-Star team in 1965. The Tigers inserted Ray Oyler at short in 1967 and moved the 27-year-old McAuliffe to second base, where he again made the All-Star team. A .247 career hitter, McAuliffe twice walked more than 100 times in a season and led the league with 95 runs in the Year of the Pitcher, 1968. He was suspended for five days that year for charging pitcher Tommy John.

Detroit won the 1968 pennant and met the St. Louis Cardinals in the World Series. Although he hit only .222 in the Series, McAuliffe scored five runs and played a flawless second base as the

Tigers won the world championship in seven games. He played shortstop in the 1972 ALCS and homered in Game 4 of the Series, won by Oakland in five games. On Oct. 23, 1973, he was traded to Boston for outfielder Ben Oglivie.

DENNY McLAIN Pitcher
Det A 1963-70, Was A 1971, Oak A 1972, Atl N 1972

Dennis Dale McLain was one of three young bonus pitchers in the White Sox organization, but only two of them could be protected on the major league roster. In spring training 1963, the Sox matched McLain against fellow bonus baby Bruce Howard in an exhibition game. When Howard won, 2-1, McLain was left unprotected. Detroit quickly drafted him. In 1965 he worked his way into the Tigers' starting rotation, making 29 starts and going 16-6.

The city of Detroit fell in love with McLain in the magical year of 1968. At the All-Star break he was 16-2. By late August he was famous. Between pitching starts, Denny appeared on the *The Ed Sullivan Show* and a host of other programs. He was featured in *Life* and *Time* as he briefly became baseball's poster boy for the younger generation. When he beat Oakland on Sept. 14, he became the first pitcher to win 30 games since 1934. McLain finished 31-6, pitching 28 complete games with a 1.96 ERA. He won both the Cy Young and the MVP Awards.

The Tigers met St. Louis in the Fall Classic. Cardinals Hall of Famer Bob Gibson had also had a great season: Although Gibson won only 22 games, his ERA was a gaudy 1.12. The two pitchers faced each other twice in the Series, and Gibson won each time, 4-0 in Game 1 and 10-1 in Game 3. But the Tigers' Mickey Lolich picked up the slack. Although McLain finally collected a victory in Game 6, Lolich won three times, beating Gibson in Game 7.

McLain followed up in 1969 by winning 24 games with a 2.80 ERA and shared the AL Cy Young with Mike Cuellar of Baltimore. Then the bottom fell out: Before the 1970 season, a story appeared in *Sports Illustrated* that linked McLain to gamblers, and Commissioner Bowie Kuhn suspended him for half the season. McLain was forced into bankruptcy and suspended twice more after his return.

Traded to the Washington Senators for as part of an eight-player deal for Joe Coleman, Aurelio Rodriguez, and Eddie Brinkman—one of the worst trades in baseball history—Denny managed to pitch 217 innings in 1971, but the results were disastrous. He lost a league-high 22 games and his arm started to fail him. McLain was out of baseball by age 30.

He went into television and radio work in Detroit, ran nightclubs, and then worked for the Class AAA Memphis Blues. When the team went under, McLain filed for bankruptcy again. In 1985 he was convicted of extortion, racketeering, and drug possession. He became a radio personality in Detroit upon release from federal prison, but he was back behind bars again in the mid-1990s for financial fraud.

JACK MORRIS Pitcher
Det A 1977-90, Min A 1991, Tor A 1992-93, Cle A 1994

Jack Morris was the type of pitcher a manager wanted on the mound with everything on the line; he almost always came through-especially in October. He went to the World Series three times with three different teams and won three world championships. With Minnesota, he was 1991 Series MVP for his masterful 10-inning shutout in Game 7 against the Atlanta Braves, one of the greatest pitching duels to ever decide a Series.

Morris broke into the starting rotation of the Tigers in 1979. He won 17 games, marking the first of 14 double-digit victory seasons. He won 162 games during the 1980s, but the only time he led the AL in wins during that decade was in strike-shortened 1981 with 14 wins. The Tigers got off to a stellar 35-5 start in 1984, including a no-hitter by Morris against the White Sox. Led by his 19 wins, Detroit captured the AL East title by 15 games. Morris breezed to an 8-1 win in the ALCS opener against Kansas City. In Games 1 and 4 of the World Series, he hurled complete-game victories over San Diego as the Tigers won in five games.

The gruff Minnesota native joined the Twins as a free agent in 1991. He made the All-Star team for the fifth time and helped the Twins become the first AL team to ever go from last place to first place in one season. Jack won twice as the Twins defeated the Toronto Blue Jays in the ALCS, then started three games in the World Series, allowing only three runs in 23 innings.

The next day Morris declared free agency. He went to Toronto, where he led the AL with 21 wins. He didn't fare well in the postseason (0-3, 7.57 ERA), though he earned his second consecutive championship ring. No longer a 200-inning workhorse, he pitched poorly for Toronto in 1993.

HAL NEWHOUSER Pitcher
Det A 1939-53, Cle A 1954-55

"Prince Hal" Newhouser is the only pitcher who ever won back-to-back MVP Awards. His dominance of the AL—going 29-9 with a 2.22 ERA in 1944 and 25-9 with a 1.81 ERA in 1945, while leading the league in strikeouts both years—is sometimes unfairly attributed to the shortage of quality players caused by World War II. But that doesn't give enough credit to Newhouser, a seasoned professional with an excellent slider who was kept out of the military by a heart condition.

Tigers scout Wish Egan took a special interest in the Detroit native, convincing Tigers management to bring Newhouser to Detroit in September 1939 despite the youngster's mixed results in the minors. In his first four full years, Newhouser went a disappointing 34-51. But after Paul Richards helped him to develop a slider, Newhouser's improvement was staggering. In the following five seasons he went 118-46, pitched 25 shutouts, led the league three times in wins and twice in ERA.

In 1945, Newhouser pitched the Tigers to a world championship, winning two of his three World Series decisions against the Cubs. Hammered in the opener, he came back to win Games 5 and 7.

Newhouser was selected to the All-Star Game seven consecutive times in the 1940s, but a sore shoulder took its toll on him by 1950. After the Tigers released the 32-year-old hurler in July 1953, Hal signed on with Cleveland in 1954, where he compiled a 7-2 record in relief for the pennant winners. He was elected to the Hall of Fame in 1992.

JIM NORTHRUP Outfield
Det A 1964-74, Mon N 1974, Bal A 1974-75

Jim Northrup was a stalwart in the Tigers' outfield in the 1960s who didn't really make news until he hit four grand slams in 1968. On June 24 that year, the lefthanded batter hit two grand slams in the same game.

Northrup became a regular for the Tigers in 1966. Two years later, he replaced an injured Al Kaline in right field, though he moved to center for the 1968 World Series. Northrup led the Tigers in the Fall Classic with eight RBIs and two home runs, including one off the Cardinals' legendary Bob Gibson. The most important one, however, was a decisive third inning grand slam that helped knot the series at three games apiece. The next year Northrup had his best season, hitting .295 with 25 homers.

LANCE PARRISH Catcher
Det A 1977-86, Phi N 1987-88, Cal A 1989-92, Sea A 1992, Cle A 1993, Pit N 1994, Tor A 1995

Through hard work and determination, Detroit's Lance Parrish made six All-Star teams and earned four Silver Slugger Awards and three Gold Gloves. Parrish impressed with his bat but struggled defensively after reaching the majors, leading the AL in passed balls in 1979 and 1980. His disagreements with Detroit manager Sparky Anderson added to his troubles: Parrish wanted to bulk up, but Anderson held to more traditional views of weight training. When Parrish's muscles paid off with homers and RBIs, however,

Anderson changed his tune. "He proved his point," Anderson admitted. "For me to criticize him now would be ignorant."

In 1982 the Tigers hired former Detroit catcher Bill Freehan to work with Parrish, with almost immediate results as Parrish was named Tiger of the Year. In the mid-1980s, Brooks Robinson said of Parrish, "All-Star catchers who average 99 RBIs and win Gold Gloves are hard to find...[Lance] is the best all-around catcher in the league."

Parrish batted .278 in the 1984 World Series as Detroit crushed San Diego. Back problems hobbled Parrish in 1986, causing him to miss half the season. Granted free agency that November, Parrish signed with the Phillies in a move that broke the owners' collusion, but he never could repeat his Detroit performances there or elsewhere. Lance later coached for the Tigers under Larry Parrish, who is no relation.

BILLY ROGELL Shortstop
Bos A 1925, 1927-28, Det A 1930-39, Chi N 1940

Slick-fielding shortstop Billy Rogell teamed with Hall of Famer Charlie Gehringer to form a smooth keystone combination for the AL-champion Tigers of 1934 and 1935. Although not noted for his batting, Rogell had 100 RBIs in 1934 as part of the best run-producing infield in history.

William George Rogell came to Detroit after washing out with the Red Sox, who tried to convert the switch hitter into a pure right-handed hitter. With the Tigers, Rogell led AL shortstops in fielding three times; in double plays twice; and in putouts, assists, and fielding range once each. Rogell played on a fractured ankle in the 1934 World Series against St. Louis, but he still managed to deliver four RBIs in Game 4. In the fourth inning of that game, it was Rogell's throw that hit pinch runner Dizzy Dean square in the head, leading to newspaper headlines that read, "X-Ray of Dean's Head Shows Nothing." The always-competitive Rogell commented: "If I'd have known his head was there, I would have thrown the ball harder."

The Tigers returned to the World Series in 1935 and were seven-game winners over the Cubs. From 1936 through 1938, Rogell batted between .274 and .276 and scored between 85 and 88 runs. When his big league days were over, Rogell managed and played in the minors until he fractured his shoulder in an auto accident. He then returned to Detroit and served for many years (until age 77) on the Detroit City Council.

MICKEY STANLEY Outfield
Det A 1964-78

One of the great defensive center fielders of the modern era, Mitchell Jack "Mickey" Stanley made no errors in both 1968 and 1970 while playing in more than 140 games each year. He won Gold Gloves in both of those seasons and also in 1969 and 1973.

Stanley was the focal point of an unusual managerial strategy in the 1968 World Series. Entering the World Series against the Cardinals, manager Mayo Smith faced a dilemma. He wanted Kaline in the lineup but had no place to put him. Jim Northrup had taken over in right field with a team-leading 90 RBIs. Left fielder Willie Horton had hit 36 home runs. Kaline didn't have enough range to play center, and besides, defense was important in Tiger Stadium's huge center field.

Then Smith had an idea. Three different Tigers had shared the shortstop position during the season; while all three could field, none could hit. In the last few weeks of the season, Smith had experimented with center fielder Stanley at short. He continued the experiment in the Series, moving Northrup from right to center and installing Kaline in right. The move paid off: Stanley made no important errors while Kaline batted .379 and drove in eight runs to help the Tigers win their first world championship since 1945.

FRANK TANANA Pitcher
Cal A 1973-80, Bos A 1981, Tex A 1982-85, Det A 1985-92, NY N 1993, NY A 1993

Frank Tanana was a classic example of a pitcher who made a successful switch from flame-thrower to finesse artist. This change allowed him to pitch in the majors for 21 years.

Tanana broke in with the Angels in 1973; he led the AL with 269 strikeouts in 1975 and paced it with a 2.54 ERA in 1977. Five years after breaking in at age 20, however, Tanana's fastball was gone. Slowed by a sore shoulder, the Angels traded him to Boston after 1980.

He came to Detroit in midseason 1985 in a contract dump by the Rangers. Durable though far from brilliant, Frank won 96 games in his seven-plus years in Motown with his minus fastball and assortment of slow curveballs. The highlight of Tanana tenure with Detroit came in 1987. The Detroit native defeated Toronto on the last day of the season, 1-0, to put the Tigers in the ALCS.

ALAN TRAMMELL Shortstop
Det A 1977-96

Only Ty Cobb and Al Kaline played more years in Detroit than Alan Trammell. At a time when the shortstop position was becoming more offense-oriented, Trammell held his own against the likes of Cal Ripken and Robin Yount. Trammell won the Gold Glove Award four times, the Silver Slugger Award three times, and was a six-time All-Star. His main attribute, though, was stability.

Trammell made his major league debut on September 9, 1977. To his left was second baseman Lou Whitaker, also making his debut. The Tigers suffered four straight losing seasons before the duo arrived; with those two as mainstays in the lineup, Detroit enjoyed 11 consecutive winning seasons, including a world championship.

Detroit rolled to a record 35-5 start in 1984. A shoulder injury cost Alan most of July, but he still hit .314 for the season and batted .364 against the Royals in a sweep of the ALCS. In crucial Game 4 of the World Series against San Diego, he homered twice with Whitaker on base to give Detroit an insurmountable three-games-to-one lead. Trammell earned Series MVP with a .450 average, five runs, two home runs, and six RBIs.

Alan's best season was 1987 when he posted career highs with a .343 average, 109 runs, 28 home runs, and 105 RBIs. He finished second to George Bell in the MVP voting, but his Tigers overtook Bell's Blue Jays on the final day of the season for the AL East title. His last All-Star season was 1990, though he continued to play in the 1990s as injuries and declining performance limited his playing time.

DIZZY TROUT Pitcher
Det A 1939-52, Bos A 1952, Bal A 1957

Paul Howard "Dizzy" Trout was a big pitcher who dominated the league for two years during World War II. He made the All-Star team twice and ended his career with a 170-161 record and a 3.23 ERA. In 1943, he went 20-12 with five shutouts; in 1944, he pitched 33 complete games and 352 innings, finishing at 27-14. His 2.12 ERA led the American League, as did his seven shutouts. He also contributed offensively, hitting .271 with five home runs and 24 RBIs.

In 1945 Trout won 18 games, including pitching six games in nine days in September to help the Tigers win the pennant. "In those days you didn't worry about sore arms or three days' rest," Trout explained. "You just kept burning them in and hoping the plate umpire had 20-20 vision."

During the World Series that year Trout pitched a five-hitter. His numbers gradually dropped off from there, though he went on to be a colorful broadcaster in Detroit. His son, Steve, became a major league pitcher for 12 seasons.

VIRGIL TRUCKS   Pitcher
Det A 1941-43, 1945-52, 1956, StL A 1953, Chi A 1953-55, KC A 1957-58, NY A 1958

For Virgil Trucks, the 1952 season was the best of times and the worst of times. The Tigers right-hander pitched two no-hitters that year, but he ended the season with a 5-19 record—the worst of his career.

Nicknamed "Fire" for his blazing fastball, Trucks was an immediate success in his rookie year, going 14-8 in 1942 and followed with a 16-10 sophomore season. He then joined the Navy and did not return to the Tigers until the last weeks of the 1945 season, just in time to win the second game of the World Series from the Cubs, 4-1.

In 1946 Trucks picked up where he had left off. A consistent winner, he had only two losing seasons during his 17-year career. Trucks played for five other major league teams, including Detroit again in 1956, before retiring with a 177-135 lifetime record.

BOBBY VEACH   Outfield
Det A 1912-23, Bos A 1924-25, NY A 1925, Was A 1925

A fine outfielder with an excellent arm and a career .310 average, Bobby Veach led the AL in RBIs three times in the 1910s. His explosive bat complemented the abilities of Tigers teammate Ty Cobb. His best season came in 1919, when the lefthanded hitter led the league in hits, doubles, and triples and batted .355 with a .519 slugging average.

Although Veach possessed good speed, which helped him in the outfield, he was reckless on the basepaths. For every successful steal he made, he was thrown out almost as often.

LOU WHITAKER   Second Base
Det A 1977-95

Lou Whitaker was great as part of an act, and he wasn't bad as a solo performer, either. The Detroit Tigers second baseman teamed with shortstop Alan Trammell for an AL record 1,918 games. Whitaker spent his entire 19-year career in Detroit, joining another Hall of Famer, Joe Morgan, as the second player to log 2,000 games at second with 2,000 hits and 200 home runs. Whitaker finished his career with a .276 average.

Lou was a third baseman his first two seasons in the minors, but was converted to second base in 1977. That September he and Trammell debuted with Detroit in the same game. "Sweet Lou" batted 285 with 61 walks to become the 1978 AL Rookie of the Year. After hitting a total of 12 home runs in his first four seasons, Whitaker smacked 15 homers and batted .286 in 1983. The next year he won the first of three straight Gold Gloves and was selected to the All-Star team for the first of five consecutive seasons. He also set a career high with a .320 average.

Whitaker's hot bat in April (.442 batting average) helped Detroit forge a 35-5 start in 1984 as the Tigers won the pennant with ease. Whitaker doubled and scored in the first inning of the World Series opener on his way to a Series-best six runs scored as the Tigers crushed San Diego.

Whitaker topped the 20-home run plateau for the first time in 1985; the following year he was part of an infield in which every player had 20 or more home runs. In 1987 Whitaker had career highs with 110 runs and 38 doubles as the Tigers came from behind to win the AL East on the season's final weekend.

In 1989, aided by an off-season conditioning program and a slightly restructured batting style, Whitaker reached career highs with 28 homers, 85 RBIs, and 89 walks. Whitaker's fielding range decreased, but his batting eye remained keen. He batted .290 or better in each of his final three seasons, including a career-best .415 on-base average at age 36 in 1993.

RUDY YORK First Base
Det A 1934, 1937-45, Bos A 1946-47, Chi A 1947, Phi A 1948

When Rudy York came to Detroit to stay in 1937, Hank Greenberg blocked his progress at first and Mickey Cochrane was in his way behind the plate. In May 1937 Cochrane was beaned and put out of action, but York still did not play regularly. Finally on Aug. 4, after the Tigers lost six straight, York was installed at catcher. He homered that day and finished with 18 homers for August, breaking Babe Ruth's record for most home runs in a month. York's 49 RBIs for the month broke the previous record set by Lou Gehrig. Rudy finished his rookie season with 35 homers and 103 RBIs.

The Tigers still didn't know where to play York. In 1938, he hit 33 homers and drove in 127 runs. Finally, in 1940 the Tigers gave Greenberg a $20,000 bonus to move to left field. That season York set career highs with a batting average of .316, a slugging average of .583, 134 RBIs, and 105 runs. Detroit won the pennant but lost to Cincinnati in the World Series. In 1943, he led the league with 34 homers and 118 RBIs but, when his production slipped, Tigers fans turned on him. He batted only .179 in the 1945 World Series and was sent to the Red Sox in January 1946, where he helped Boston win the pennant with his sixth season of more than 100 RBIs.

Tigers 1999-2000

WHEELING AND DEALING

Since Randy Smith took over in November 1995, he has made 46 trades through the Juan Gonzalez deal. That's an average of almost one trade per month, including the 23 trades he made in 1996 alone!

Smith came to Detroit after spending two and a half years as GM of the San Diego Padres. Since then, Smith has made seven trades with his former club, including four in the year after he left. Smith's father, Tal, is the longtime president of the Houston Astros; that connection has produced four trades, including seven-player and nine-player deals. Of the 46 trades Smith has made while in Detroit, 27 have been with NL clubs.

To put in perspective just how dramatically different the Smith regime has been, consider that it took the team nine years to make the previous 46 trades before Smith took over. Consider also that Smith has made more trades in four years than the Tigers made in the first half of the 20th century (43 trades total from 1901-51). That comparison ignores the drastic changes in the game since 1951, but it does show nicely how relentlessly Smith has made personnel moves.

The blockbuster November deal with Texas perhaps signaled that Smith understood that he had to build an AL team, not an NL team, if he was going to prosper in Detroit.

BEST CASE 2000

Randy Smith regains his genius laurels as Detroit celebrates the opening of Comerica Park with a Wild Card berth and the team plays its first meaningful October games in more than a decade. MVP candidate Juan Gonzalez bashes 40-50 homers and drives in 125-plus runs, leading the Tigers back into contention in their new playground. With solid seasons from infielders Clark, Easley, and Palmer, and with outfielders Higginson and Encarnacion bouncing back from off years, the Bengals' fearsome lineup bashes opponents into submission. Matt Anderson harnesses his 100 mph heater and develops into a dominating closer, anchoring a solid bullpen. Detroit's big bats make a mediocre rotation anchored by veteran Dave Mlicki (who received a long-term deal after his solid '99 performance) and sophomore Jeff Weaver good enough to keep the club in contention throughout the season.

WORST CASE 2000

An unhappy Gonzalez doesn't get the megabucks long-term deal he expects, has a good—but not great—year on the field, and is a disruptive force in the clubhouse. If the outfield fails to improve and the starting rotation struggles, the inaugural season at the new park might be a rough one.

PROSPECTS

Trying to re-energize the major league club, Smith used **OF GABE KAPLER, RHP FRANCISCO CORDERO,** and **LHP ALAN WEBB**, three of the top young players in the system, to lure Juan Gonzalez from Texas. Cordero rebounded from an injury-filled '98 to return to form and the All-Prospect Team. Kapler was a member of that team in 1998. Webb, the youngest pitcher in the Double-A Southern League, had a bright first half before slumping in the second half.

Detroit believes it has the position players to compete but must upgrade its pitching. Many of the highly touted pitchers have not lived up to early expectations, at least not yet. The team's 1996 first-round pick **RHP SETH GREISINGER** went down early last season with elbow problems. Detroit's 1997 first-round pick **RHP MATT ANDERSON** had all kinds of command problems and was shipped back to the minor leagues. Japanese import **RHP MASADA KIDA** did not perform as advertised.

On the minor league level, **RHP MATT DREWS** and **RHP MIKE DRUM-RIGHT**, two former first-rounders whom the organization counted on to anchor the rotation, have combined for a 17-62 record and an ERA over 7.00 the last two years. The Tigers gave up on Drumright, shipping him to the Marlins in a minor league deal July 31. **RHP WILLIS ROBERTS**, another high-octane arm, posted a 6.26 ERA.

The trade of Cordero and Webb seriously cuts into the organization's young pitching depth. 1998 first-round pick **RHP JEFF WEAVER** had an outstanding first half. **RHP DAVE BORKOWSKI**, a big winner on the minor league level, received some valuable big league experience. **RHP VICTOR SANTOS** has a chance, as do **RHP SHANE LOUX, RHP NATE CORNEJO,** and **LHP ADAM PETTYJOHN** further down, but each is years away.

Behind the plate the organization has a quality hitter in **C ROB FICK,** added another big stick in the '99 draft with **1B-C ERIC MUNSON,** and got a big season from **C JAVIER CARDONA,** but the everyday ranks are thinning out. **OF CHRIS WAKELAND** has a potent bat, but his defense needs an upgrade and he's already 25. **OF RICHARD GOMEZ** is a fine hitter, has great speed and a chance to add power, but he's several years away.

UNDER THE MICROSCOPE

ROBERT FICK

A shoulder problem kept Fick out most of last season, but he returned in time to hit the last home run in Tiger Stadium history, a grand slam. Fick is a hitting machine, having won MVP honors in the Class-A Midwest League in '97 before hitting .318 with 114 RBIs in '98 at Double A. The lefthanded swinger hit a combined 97 doubles over the two seasons. Can Fick's build and defensive shortcomings hold up on an everyday basis behind the plate? Because of the injury, the Tigers will have to wait until this season to find the answer.

ERIC MUNSON

The Tigers need Munson, their '99 first-round pick, to move quickly. An advanced hitter with power potential, the USC product could fill a power void from the left side at Comerica park in the near future, perhaps 2001. A collegiate catcher, Munson would prefer to stay there but he may lack the defensive tools, and the organization doesn't want to compromise his offensive potential.

DAVID BORKOWSKI

The Michigan native realized his dream of playing for his home-state team in 1999 and gained valuable experience as a starter and as a reliever. The 23-year-old has won big at the minor league level, displaying a lively arm and sinking fastball, and he should get an opportunity in either role this season.

ADAM PETTYJOHN

The 1998 second-round draft pick pitched well at both the Class-A and Double-A levels in 1999, winning 14 times. Featuring a good slider and two fastballs, Pettyjohn should contribute at the major league level, but won't be ready this season.